Becoming more Agile whilst delivering Salesforce

What readers are saying

"Simplifies game-changing concepts from the tech industry, bringing them to life with tangible examples and making them applicable to all industries and organisations. It is an impactful and accessible book full of practical tips that will have immediate and significant impact. It's refreshing and inspiring to see that values of the author coming through so strongly, and the emphasis on personal leadership and self improvement is empowering."

Claire Fox, Chief Operating Officer UNICEF UK

"This book was a joy to read. Ines has a wonderful style of writing and uses stories, quotes and tips to great effect! The audience of this books is wider than Salesforce and includes anyone wanting to build great products with teams of people."

Seb Chakraborty, Group CTO Goco (GoCompare)

"Ines translates her deep and broad experience and wisdom of Agile concepts into workable tips and actionable practices, promoting a practical and effective application of Agile in the Salesforce domain. This book is a must read for anyone even considering attempting Agile with Salesforce."

Don Robins, Salesforce Training Partner & MVP

Becoming more Agile whilst delivering Salesforce

Practical tips and experiments to start using today!

by Ines Garcia

Becoming more Agile whilst delivering Salesforce
Practical tips and experiments to start using today!
Ines Garcia

Published by Get Agile Ltd, www.getagile.co.uk
A record for this book is available from the British Library.

Ebook ISBN: 978-1-8381631-0-5
Print ISBN: 978-1-8381631-6-7

To every trailblazer, to you.

Find where there is no path, and leave a trail.

Table of Contents

Foreword
by Geoff Watts

When I was a young project manager, I was lucky enough to be given access to training courses to learn all sorts of new skills. These training courses varied from computer based training modules, to classroom lectures delivered by experts, to self-guided distance learning and other formats. By far and away the training that stuck with me the most were the ones that used story-telling, and in particular stories told by people who had not done things perfectly.

I remember being captivated by narrative of real-life examples of moments in projects that I could readily identify with. I realised immediately that what I was learning was relevant to me and I was not alone in facing these examples of imperfection.

Ines is a storyteller at heart and in this book manages to share some difficult to understand and difficult to accept messages in a very relatable way. She writes as if she is talking to you without patronising because she has seen and experienced all of the challenges she describes first hand.

I was unsure as to whether I was the right person to write a foreword for a book about Salesforce as I have no personal experience of the product. How could I vouch for something written about a product I do not know? Well, after reading it, it turns out I didn't need to know about Salesforce because the challenges are very similar to the challenges that I have faced in other industries.

Ines has managed to explain the challenges, and techniques to tackle them, in a way that will be very useful to everyone working with Salesforce while simultaneously not excluding people working on other configurable products and services or even in-house upgrades or rewrites.

The principles behind the manifesto for agile software development have been a useful guide for over twenty years now and, as principles, they deliberately avoid giving specific demands for how to do our work. They provide a form of professional moral compass and leave the interpretation to us. This is both liberating and daunting. When there are limitless options, how do we know what to do?

Well there is no right answer and we learn through trial and error and experience. But that experience does not have to be our own. I have always been a big fan of learning from other people's mistakes and experiences to minimise my own pain so if I was starting out on a Salesforce-based project I would love to take Ines' years of experience and use it as a short-cut to my own success. I recommend you do too.

Geoff Watts,
Agile Leadership Coach, Inspect & Adapt, Author

Scrum Mastery:
From Good to Great Servant-Leadership

Product Mastery:
From Good to Great Product Ownership

Team Mastery:
From Good to Great Agile Teamwork

The Coach's Casebook:
Mastering The Twelve Traits That Trap Us

Foreword

by Mary Scotton

In my 2nd year as a Platform Product Manager, designing point & click tools for non-programmers to customize and build enterprise apps, Salesforce shifted from waterfall to Agile methodology. It was 2006 and I'd just written a STUNNING 50 page manifesto (aka functional spec) for sControl "2.0". The shift to Agile meant, "Sorry, Mary, we don't write functional specs anymore". My world crumbled a little (ok, a lot...). What was my PURPOSE? How would I communicate my ideas? Would I still have a JOB?

We made the shift. And I still had a job -- an even broader one. I became the leader of a cross-functional team (no more tossing specs over the wall to developers!). We had daily standups. I shared my ideas verbally, collaborating with my new teammates by writing on whiteboards. And playing ping-pong. We bonded as a team, with a common goal (to this day, these are the folks I remember most fondly!). We set monthly "sprint" goals. We started sprint reviews, sharing our progress with the whole Platform team, and getting feedback.

Over time, we went from 1 major release a year to 3 major releases a year. I forgot about those long functional specs and got good at writing User Stories (As a < type of user >, I want < some goal > so that < some reason >.). Today, I still use that formula to organize my thoughts. For example, I apply it to making tech communities more inclusive: "As a transgender person at a tech conference, I want people to know my pronouns so that when I network it isn't awkward." The resulting "product" in this example is pronoun buttons for all attendees and education for cisgender people about the user story.

For me, transitioning to Agile was big and scary. I wish I'd had this book then! Ines distills the big ideas into small steps and this guide is immediately actionable — just try any of the "Why not try…" experiments! I enjoy Ines' conversational style and realistic approach. Her years of experience come through in the real-world examples and lay the foundation for understanding the Agile principles. And, Ines' underlying message of "come on people, we should have FUN and ENJOY this life!" reminds me to slow down and be grateful for the incredible community of people like Ines that I've had the pleasure to meet on my journey. Read on, and have fun!

Mary Scotton,
Technology Industry Leader - Making Tech & Tech Communities Inclusive

Patent Holder:
Multiple Salesforce Platform low-code tool inventions

Speaker & Writer:
Hacking the Tech Workforce

Keynote Speaker:
Salesforce, Salesforce Community, and Industry Tech Conferences

Introduction

Why am I writing this book? This question has been on my mind since I started writing it. On reflection, I believe the answer is:

Because I care to share that life doesn't have to be that painful!

Intrinsically, we humans want to be happy. Happiness derives from having a purpose, i.e. the pursuit of that interesting and challenging 'something' that is greater than oneself.

I have been in the Salesforce ecosystem since 2013. Time and time again I see deliveries being consistently late, projects taking way too long, or projects with then dissatisfied customers, organisations that can't seem to deliver within their budgets, problems with the quality of the work once deployed, stressed teams and all around unhappy people.

Life is perishable and it's not worth living it like this.

The emotional and mental states of each of us go hand in hand. We spend a big chunk of our lives working, a place where we should enable that pursuit of happiness. After all, motivation is partially derived from the feeling of a job well done.

"Success is liking yourself, liking what you do, and liking how you do it." - Maya Angelou[1]

Just because something 'has always been that way' does not mean it is a good way nor that it has to continue that way. *You*

---

1   Maya Angelou, "Oxford Essential Quotations: Maya Angelou", Oxford Reference, https://www.oxfordreference.com/view/10.1093/oi/authority.20110803095413146

can change things. Don't accept the status quo. After all, each one of us is the creative force of our own life!

In the same instance businesses must change things and reject the status quo, else leaves little to no room for innovation or improvement. The ability to inspect and adapt constantly enables an organisation to succeed but, more importantly, is a must for survival. The findings of a McKinsey study[2] were that 17% of IT projects go so badly that they can threaten the very existence of a company, with a range of budget overruns of more than 200% - 400%.

The good news is that there's light at the end of the tunnel… There is a better way, and it's not all that new and flashy, in fact it's been around for more than twenty years. Since its inception, its ethos has been to make work more humane.

"… We all felt privileged to work with a group of people who held a set of compatible values, a set of values based on trust and respect for each other and promoting organizational models based on people, collaboration, and building the types of organizational communities in which we would want to work. At the core, …[this is]… about delivering good products to customers by operating in an environment that does more than talk about 'people as our most important asset' but actually 'acts' as if people were the most important, and loses the word 'asset'."[3]

So I'd like to share this *better way* with you so that you can share it with your team and environment and like the law of critical mass[4], it can become an unstoppable snowball effect.

---

2   Michael Bloch, Sven Blumberg and Jürgen Laartz, "Delivering large-scale IT projects on time, on budget, and on value", Mckinsey, 1/October/12, https://www.mckinsey.com/

3   Jim Highsmith, "History: The Agile Manifesto", Agile Manifesto, 2001, https://agilemanifesto.org/history.html

4   Pamela Oliver, Gerald Marwell and Ruy Teixeira, "A Theory of the Critical Mass. I. Interdependence, Group Heterogeneity, and the Production of Collective Action", *American Journal of Sociology*, Vol. 91, No. 3 (1985): pp. 522-556, https://www.jstor.org

Especially within the Salesforce Ecosystem[5] as this is where I invest most of my time and effort today, with an incredible community of professionals who share and help each other beyond their way. So throughout this book we'll look at every step, every bit and piece, through the lens of Salesforce. Yet an Agile mindset works in many contexts!

> For those who have found themselves with this book and haven't heard of Salesforce, please reach out and let me know how you ended up with it? Seriously, I'm curious!
>
> A quick description: *Salesforce.com, Inc. is an American cloud-based software company headquartered in San Francisco, California. It provides customer-relationship management service and also sells a complementary suite of enterprise applications focused on customer service, marketing automation, analytics, and application development.*[6]
>
> As an Agile Coach and Salesforce MVP[7], I help companies to become more Agile whilst delivering Salesforce solutions. Admittedly, I very much enjoy *playing* with the technology at the same time.
>
> A quick tip then, for those who are just learning about Salesforce, to make more sense of this book's content. Do this: every time you encounter [Salesforce] here onwards just change the word to whichever industry you are involved with. Tada!

---

5   Laura Fagan, "The Salesforce Ecosystem Explained", Salesforce, 1/September/15, https://www.salesforce.com/

6   "Salesforce", Wikipedia, https://en.wikipedia.org/wiki/Salesforce

7   A Salesforce MVP is a title as part of a program for Salesforce to showcase individuals in their ecosystem for their knowledge about the products and involvement with their community.

If you are not delivering software/digital solutions you can also change the words [software] or [code] to [product] everytime you encounter them.

One thing worth mentioning for everybody reading is that you don't have to read it all in one go. There are multiple chapters and sections within each. Please allow yourself and your environment to digest and experiment with its content. This is where the real benefit lies.

There is no rush as such, we already know that 'big bang' approaches can be dangerous.

"There's more to life than increasing its speed" - Mahatma Gandhi[8]

Just going faster doesn't lead us to a better destination. The grand difference between efficiency and effectiveness, right? We must work smart, not just hard.

As per the title of this book, this is about *being*; a process, a journey 'to be' instead of 'to do'. In today's fast-paced world, it is easy to grow accustomed to always thinking about what's going to happen next. In my experience, the difference lies in a mindset, *being* meaning a journey and focusing on the principles that guide our acts.

An evolution—not a revolution—from wherever you may be now to gradually getting closer to where you want to be.

I came across both Salesforce and Agile at more or less the same time. When working on business transformations, digital solutions have a lot to do with it. Technology can really be the enabler to support that evolution, but it doesn't do much by itself.

---

8   Mahatma Gandhi, quoted by Susan Ratcliffe, *Oxford Essential Quotations,* 5 ed. (Oxford: Oxford University Press, 2017), https://www.oxfordreference.com/

A side note about semantics: *transformation* is a heavy word and to some may sound scary, I much prefer to use *evolution* as it has connotations of developing gradually and, ideally, organically.

After all, the gradual approach is what Agile is all about: incremental, step-by-step change, evolution not revolution.

The word 'agile' has been misunderstood and misused as an excuse for pressure, poor product and performance and an attempt at a selling point… Sadly, because of this, it comes with a lot of baggage.

So let's start with a blank canvas.

We need to bear in mind how our human brains process new concepts[9]: The human brain tries to understand a new idea by applying the old ones into it. No wonder things get so mixed up!

Right, so you have already committed the time to read this book, and for that I thank you. Now I am asking you for even more: from this page onwards, try your hardest to forget what you have learnt about Agile and join me in discovering a mindset that says **life can be better** whilst delivering Salesforce or whatever you do, whether it's related to work or not.

Ready?

Let's go!

---

9   CrashCourse, "Cognition - How Your Brain Can Amaze and Betray You: Crash Course Psychology #15", YouTube, 19/May/14, https://www.youtube.com/watch?v=R-sVnmmw6WY

How to Read this Book

Throughout the next chapters we'll cover the Agile Principles, and we'll do so through a Salesforce lens; and in each one you will find the following sections:

Story

A story to get us in the mood for the chapter and provide some context. It's worth noting that all stories in this book are based on real life scenarios, the names and some of the details have been tweaked to preserve the anonymity of the individuals, teams and organisations involved.

Tip

Tips are a few practical bits of advice that I have picked up along the way over my Salesforce and Agile professional career. Take note as these parts will provide guidance about the subject at hand.

Why not try...

These are experiments, things for you to try.

Take them as challenges and don't try them all at once!

Semantics

I believe the words we use play a big part in all of this, with small conscious tweaks about using some instead of others can and do make a difference to how the same content is digested differently by the recipients.

Book

I read a lot, well I used to read a lot, I have for the last couple of years picked up that habit again with pleasure. The 'Book' section is a brief mention of books that I recommend for future reading which are related to the subject at hand. I'm sure there are more and I'd be quite interested to hear your suggestions! #SalesforceAgile

A word of caution:

"Reading, after a certain age, diverts the mind too much from its creative pursuits. Any man who reads too much and uses his own brain too little falls into lazy habits of thinking." - Albert Einstein[10]

So if or when your mind starts to wander, that's okay. Close the book and explore the thoughts that it has triggered. Come back later.

---

10   Albert Einstein, quoted in an interview with George Sylvester Viereck, "What Life Means to Einstein", *Saturday Evening Post*, 26/October/29; re-printed in George Sylvester Viereck, *Glimpses of the Great.* (New York: The Macaulay company, 1930)

A Bit of Foundation

The scaffolding that I used to structure the content of the following chapters is based on a simple format: The Agile Principles[11].

To me, the only way to make sense of all this 'agile hype' is to understand the underlying principles, the only way to make it 'click', rather than the unfortunate common mistake of 'going through the motions without emotions' which would make it fragile rather than agile.

Before we get to it, some light background history:

Last century we, the working world, focused more on execution than on innovation. We were clear on what we wanted to accomplish and exactly how people were going to deliver it. Think about mass production. Very defined modules, roles, processes and practices, all to deliver detailed plans. It made sense.

Now things are evolving rapidly as we live in an ever-changing environment. Let's be honest, the only constant is change. To stay competitive we need to inspect and adapt faster to deal with greater uncertainty. Only organisations that learn will keep up with the future.

You may be asking yourself: what does the word 'agile' have to do with all of this? Well, allow me to tell you the brief story of how it came about. Once upon a time...

---

11   Jim Highsmith, "Principles behind the Agile Manifesto", Agile Manifesto, 2001, https://agilemanifesto.org/principles.html

In 2001, some representatives[12] of XP, DSDM, Crystal, ASD, FDD, Scrum (these were, back then, a radical new wave of approaches for running software projects) and more gathered and put their discrepancies aside to look at the similarities at the core of their practices. The outcome of this event was the Agile Manifesto[13].

The concept of being agile is not new. It's been around for more than twenty years when technologists started doing things differently to traditional project management methodologies.

Acronyms are dangerous as they can be both misunderstood and misused, so I do try to avoid them. If you ask me, acronyms can be defined as: error-prone abbreviations. So let's briefly describe those above:

- XP - **Extreme Programming** is an Agile software development framework that aims to produce higher quality software, and a higher quality of life for the development team. XP is the most specific of the Agile frameworks regarding appropriate engineering practices for software development.[14]

- DSDM - **Dynamic Systems Development Method** is an Agile project delivery framework, initially used as a software development method. First released in 1994, DSDM originally sought to provide some discipline to the Rapid Application Development (RAD) method.[15]

---

12   Jim Highsmith, "The Agile Manifesto", Agile Manifesto, 2001, https://agilemanifesto.org/

13   Jim Highsmith, "The Agile Manifesto", Agile Manifesto, 2001, https://agilemanifesto.org

14   Don Wells, "Extreme Programming", Agile Alliance, 2013, https://www.agilealliance.org/glossary/xp/

15   "Dynamic systems development method", Wikipedia, https://en.wikipedia.org/wiki/Dynamic_systems_development_method

- **Crystal** (not an acronym, but worth clarifying) - Several of the key tenets of Crystal include teamwork, communication and simplicity, as well as reflection to frequently adjust and improve the process.[16]

- ASD - **Adaptive Software Development** is a software development process that embodies the principle that continuous adaptation of the process to the work at hand is the normal state of affairs, with a repeating series of speculation, collaboration, and learning cycles.[17]

- FDD - **Feature-Driven Development** is an iterative, lightweight and incremental process for developing software. Is driven from a client-valued functionality (feature) perspective. Its main purpose is to deliver tangible, working software repeatedly in a timely manner.[18]

- **Scrum** (not an acronym either but let's clarify) - Today Scrum refers to a lightweight framework that is used to deliver complex, innovative products and services to truly delight customers. It is simple to understand, but difficult to master.[19]

Even Salesforce themselves made the move from more traditional development to becoming more agile, an initiative that started in 2006 with their engineering team. With that move

16   "Crystal Methods", Wikiversity, https://en.wikiversity.org/wiki/Crystal_Methods

17   "What is Adaptive Software Development (ASD)?", Product Plan, https://www.productplan.com/glossary/adaptive-software-development/

18   "Feature-driven development", Wikipedia, https://en.wikipedia.org/wiki/Feature-driven_development

19   "Definition of Scrum", Scrum Alliance, https://www.scrumalliance.org/about-scrum/definition

they managed to wrap up their major product releases 60% faster![20] That's a big number.

Going back to the Agile Manifesto, you first encounter the following:

"We are uncovering better ways of developing
software by doing it and helping others do it.
Through this work we have come to value:

Individuals and interactions over processes and tools
Working software over comprehensive documentation
Customer collaboration over contract negotiation
Responding to change over following a plan

That is, while there is value in the items on
the right, we value the items on the left more."[21]

The values of the Agile Manifesto.

---

20   Chad Holdorf, "Introducing Agile Accelerator: How You Can Manage Agile Development Through Salesforce", Salesforce, 24/April/15, https://www.salesforce.com/blog/2015/04/introducing-agile-accelerator.html

21   Mike Beedle et al., "The Agile Manifesto", Agile Manifesto, 2001, https://agilemanifesto.org

I particularly like the weighting or comparison in the values itself. Unlike values in other theories, practices, organisations etc. where they are displayed as a set of adjectives. Here as you can see that is within some sort of context, and each value is relative rather than absolute.

Let's briefly break each one down by highlighting boldly the importance of that weighting.

Individuals and interactions over processes and tools.

Of course there are processes and tools, we are not talking about anarchy here! But rather than a control forced upon people, to me this tells us where the real value is found and that's within individuals and interactions. Meaning who is involved and how do they relate to each other. We are not 'interchangeable resource items', we must recognise the value and importance of people as individuals rather than as assets.

"The performance of a system is not the sum of its parts. It's the PRODUCT of its INTERACTIONS." – Dr. Russell L. Ackoff[22]

A system? Yes! Groups, teams and organisations are operating systems! Think about it. Their architecture, how they are modularised, the properties of both elements and relations and the

22   Dr. Russell Ackoff, "A Lifetime of Systems Thinking", The Systems Thinker, https://thesystemsthinker.com/a-lifetime-of-systems-thinking/

quantity and quality of their interactions have an enormous impact on the performance of the system as a whole. We could just call it *synergy:* the creation of a whole that is greater than the simple sum of its parts.[23]

Modular system architecture is not just for software development. We can observe it in nature and see how work should be: performing in specialised grouplets whilst working together as a whole.

"We want to restore a balance" - Agile Manifesto[24]

And to do so, we have much to undo, years of imposition and conformity of rules and controls, that suppress creativity, curiosity and energy.

Working software over comprehensive documentation.

Let's just nip this in the bud, one of the biggest misconceptions I come across is that agile teams don't have documentation. In fact, they DO! It is very naive to think: "no documentation, of course they go faster".

To me this value is reinforcing the vision, the 'why are we even here?', the finished product increment is what counts as the main result of every iteration, that is what we primarily measure ourselves against. We could think of documentation as a byproduct.

Let's be honest, long-winded documentation produced at the very end becomes stale and outdated by the time it gets finished. It's an incredibly draining exercise for all parties involved. And who actually reads this documentation, anyway?

Then of course the pursuit is to have self explanatory code which is very important, it's a journey rather than a destina-

23   "Synergy", Wikipedia, https://en.wikipedia.org/wiki/Synergy

24   Mike Beedle et al., "The Agile Manifesto", Agile Manifesto, 2001, https://agilemanifesto.org

tion, where anyone could understand its use. And when I say anyone I mean it, non-developers too.

Commenting code is often a practice to explain areas where there may be more complexity, although the aim is to 'Keep It Simple'. The most valuable source comments are the ones that clarify the developer's intent and why they chose to do something in a certain way. In other words, it's the "why", not the "how". Yet even with easy-to-understand code and comments, it's difficult to grasp the context of the whole.

I am diverging here a little bit with all this documentation talk, let's wrap it up:

- Documentation is not a step on a linear timeline, and certainly not the one at the end.

- It is ongoing, constantly.

- Keep it simple and modular.

- The way and tools to use for documenting is for the team to decide, whichever works best in their environment.

- It should be accessible and understandable by the organisation, it's your institutional knowledge.

One way (not the only way) that I have seen this working quite well is having an online one pager describing functionality with the following sections:

1. Business Reason: the aim, the why we even invest time and effort on this.

2. Architecture: representation of the physical data model[25].

3. UI flow Diagram: modeling the logic, interactions and paths that users/systems can have.

---

25   "What is a Physical Data Model?", Techopedia, https://www.techopedia.com/definition/30600/physical-data-model

4. Discarded Options: why not another solution? As there is always more than one way to achieve something.

5. Approval Process: who to contact about this functionality, when might one be interested to enhance it or extend it.

To finish on this, although there is value in documentation for many reasons our primary measure is the working finished product.

"We embrace documentation, but not hundreds of pages of never-maintained and rarely-used tomes. " - Agile Manifesto[26]

Customer collaboration over contract negotiation.

Earlier I mentioned that nowadays things change really fast. That includes the Salesforce world with three major releases[27] a year, big announcements at the annual conference Dreamforce[28] (the biggest software conference on the planet as of this writing) and their acquisition rate[29].

With all of that change, you need to add your own organisation, industry, market, stock, the world… The list of changing factors is endless. Things that seem important now can easily become obsolete tomorrow and things that we may have not even thought about yet could be a deal breaker for industry survival.

---

26   Mike Beedle et al., "The Agile Manifesto", Agile Manifesto, 2001, https://agilemanifesto.org

27   "Salesforce Release Readiness Strategies", Trailhead Salesforce, https://trailhead.salesforce.com/en/content/learn/modules/sf_releases

28   "Dreamforce 2019", Dreamforce, https://www.salesforce.com/dreamforce/

29   "Salesforce", Crunchbase, https://www.crunchbase.com/organization/salesforce/acquisitions/acquisitions_list

On this uncertain basis, there is no point in concentrating or focusing time and effort on 'the four corners'[30]. Instead let's divert that intelligence and energy to working together towards the common goal.

With synergy across the whole organisation.

You may be thinking, "but contracts are *serious stuff*! It's not that easy or up to us to change". To keep your legal team happy, over time the way that you craft contracts will evolve to support this. And do this in synergy with who pays the bills and who is actually consuming the product at the end of the day.

As things change quickly, working together day in and day out is where the value lies in order to produce a working product that people actually want, instead of a back-and-forth clerical burden. By this, I mean the especially routine chores like reporting that no one actually looks at, meetings about meetings, administrative tasks etc.

Declutter to minimize waste and come together for the common goal. We've heard about scope creep but there is also *bureaucracy* creep.

"We embrace modeling, but not in order to file some diagram in a dusty corporate repository." - Agile Manifesto[31]

Responding to change over following a plan.

Having a path for the product is good, building that non-linear path *in line* with the vision is key and doing it together 'makes it or breaks it'. Tuning and adjusting it as we go and learning from it is what wins in an ever-changing environment.

I'm sorry to break this to you ... we can't predict the future.

---

30 "Four corners (law)", Wikipedia, https://en.wikipedia.org/wiki/Four_corners_(law)

31 Mike Beedle et al., "The Agile Manifesto", Agile Manifesto, 2001, https://agilemanifesto.org

Having upfront detailed plans about the predicted sequence of events in detail to build something in a complex environment is project suicide. It looks something like:

When in fact, at the point in time of starting a project is when we know the least we are ever going to know. Having small cycles with constant feedback loops enables you to keep time, budget and quality fixed, while continuously learning and adapting the product as you go and as you learn.

The value is found in being adaptable, with a deep understanding that new things will emerge and supersede others, it's part of nature. Reduce waste then; stop draining time, effort and energy trying to define a linear detailed future upfront.

"We plan, but recognize the limits of planning in a turbulent environment." - Agile Manifesto[32]

---

32   Mike Beedle et al., "The Agile Manifesto", Agile Manifesto, 2001, https://agilemanifesto.org

A *fun* note to wrap up the chapter:

We talked about how there is a better way to look at projects, an alternative. But an alternative to what?

Well, 'the other', more traditional (or olden days in my opinion) way to look at delivering projects is most often used and referred to as the waterfall model.

That model being a sequential (non-iterative) design process, in which progress is seen as flowing steadily downwards through the phases of:

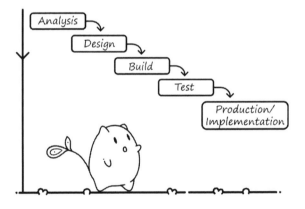

A cascade of events.

And I won't argue that for simple stuff, a waterfall approach works well, you know what to produce and exactly how to, there is no uncertainty there nor lack of agreement. Go for it.

The waterfall approach is often attributed to Dr Winston Royce. What I find quite amusing is that even he, in his paper 'Proceedings IEEE' from 1970[33] where the model was introduced, says:

"I believe in this concept but the implementation described above is risky and invites failure."[34]

Ha! Apparently no one read that far...

"We want to restore a balance. We embrace modeling, but not in order to file some diagram in a dusty corporate repository. We embrace documentation, but not hundreds of pages of never-maintained and rarely-used tomes. We plan, but recognize the limits of planning in a turbulent environment." - Agile Manifesto[35]

---

33   IEEE History Center Staff, "Proceedings of the IEEE Through 100 Years: 1970-1979 [Scanning Our Past]", Proceedings of the IEEE, vol. 100, no. 8, 2012: pp. 2555-2567, https://ieeexplore.ieee.org/document/6239653

34   Winston W. Royce, "Managing the Development of Large Software Systems", Technical Papers of Western Electronic Show and Convention (WesCon), 1970, Los Angeles, USA.

35   Mike Beedle et al., "The Agile Manifesto", Agile Manifesto, 2001, https://agilemanifesto.org

Deliver Value Early and Constantly

"Our highest priority is to satisfy the customer through early and continuous delivery of valuable software." - Agile Manifesto[36]

---

36   Mike Beedle et al., "The Agile Manifesto", Agile Manifesto, 2001, https://agilemanifesto.org

Pull Out All the Stops

"Take a good look around this table. We are the first cross-functional team this company has ever put together and we are going to show everyone a new way of doing things. With newness there is inevitably some uncertainty. The beauty of uncertainty is that it also provides excitement and opportunity."

Siobhan, the Product Owner, was buzzing as she addressed the team. Up to this point, teams within the company had been made up of groups of people working on the same things, in the same way, with the same skills, reporting and working within established sequences and protocols. Her team featured people from all areas; Jaime, the data engineer, Mike, from Salesforce development, Gabby, who had forgotten more than Siobhan would ever know about AWS, Sarb, with her React Native knowledge and Moyo from e-commerce. They'd be joined by third party vendors shortly. There was a sense of anticipation around the table and everyone's eagerness to be involved in something new and ground-breaking was palpable.

"If we make this work," continued Siobhan, "we won't just improve sales, we'll be proactive in servicing; providing solutions for customers before they even know that they have a problem. Pretty cool, eh?"

"This all sounds great, boss. What's our process?" Jaime, ever rigid, wanted to know.

"Our process is fluid. That's what's wonderful about being a cross-functional team; we can work efficiently and spontaneously, as required. We can work in whatever order and partnership functions best at any stage of product development. We have to make sense of multiple data feeds from all the company's products. How do we do that? By having multiple skill-sets on our team - particularly you, Jaime. We have to intelligently group our customers. Who knows our customers best? Moyo. We need to use this data to personalise the way we communicate with customers - Mike, Gabby, Sarb, that's you. Working in this way allows us to bypass clunky processes and react to the needs of our particular project. Adding to these human benefits, we can make use of AI and machine learning so that customers can see information most relevant to them; we can provide true personalisation."

As Siobhan continued to explain how they would all work together in a web of communication, they got more and more excited. Even Jaime, who could see that working in this multidisciplinary way would allow her to refine her contributions, contribute more efficiently and expand her knowledge.

Through continued communication and by making the most of their autonomy to work differently the team built a structure for handling the rules to show information. They built new rules and elevated parts of the architecture to more easily amend some of the logic, for example the threshold to determine how active a customer is in their mobile app, or to add a new variable into a collection of customer group types. This enabled tweaks to be faster, easier and less painful.

As time went on, the team continued working on extending logic and adding new data feeds as well as more channels to surface the information in. They got used to the new way of working and were energised by how little time was wasted waiting for different departments to do their bit; they were a fully-functioning, self-contained unit.

It became clear, however, that the barriers between their unit and the rest of the company weren't as permeable as they'd hoped. They were producing great work, but nothing was happening with it. Their new way of doing things was saving time from start to end, but getting their products outside the company walls was still taking as long as ever.

Siobhan's team had overcome the staid, old-fashioned way of doing things, but she still had to work within that structure outside of her team, so overall, nothing was getting speeded up. Small ideas they had weren't going to market and getting tested because, although her team was working well, the old barriers still existed between them and the customers.

"I've had this functionality ready for weeks," fretted Sarb, "and only now it needs changing? I could have done this ages ago!" The team were starting to worry that the time now elapsing from the inception of ideas to their actual use was becoming too great; their product was still not yet being used. In the long run, that means more waste and more effort to fine tune the product. This also means more cost, which is one of the things the creation of a cross-functional team was hoping to avoid.

As a result, the last couple of weeks of the project were particularly intense; and naturally then new ideas emerged. The project picked up speed again and finally, with smaller feedback loops engendered by the team, could flourish once more.

The thing is, the work that we do is quite conceptual. What I mean with that is that we create more than we recreate or duplicate. We transform from concept to tangible outcomes, screens, response, data processing … That is also true for other goods such as architecture, music, art etc. Unlike physical products, which we can see, smell, and touch; software is in a sense intangible. There is more room for variety and creativity, and it is harder to imagine what the final outcome will look like. Oftentimes, we only realise what we want and what we don't want after we see the final product.

Slicing work can help, so that you can show that tangible outcome in small chunks and so that it can be used. As the work is so conceptual, being able to see it helps to redefine constantly and reduce deviation. How you "slice" the work makes the difference in delivering often, let's say in days/weeks not months. That allows you to have that value in use already! That is super powerful!

With sliced work you can then have small delivery cycles and feedback loops, that enables you to:

- Go to market earlier
- Get income/return of investment sooner
- Get feedback earlier
- Tune & adjust for what is really wanted
- Reduce waste

Whatever it is you're working on, break it down, *real down*. So that it's easier to estimate, to deliver and to validate its effort. Doing so it also helps the team to wrap their head around it.

Delivering value is not just getting something done, it's only when it's used and cared for by consumers when it becomes of value. And I refer to consumers over customers, clients, stake-holders… as to whom consumes whatever it is that has been delivered. We must be results-oriented. If the product is not used, then it has no value.

In line with the concept of breaking it down, let's not forget about deploying in small batches. Doing so reduces the frequency of deployment errors, easier to debug and troubleshoot, so that fixes and updates can be tested and released quickly; which ultimately eases continuous delivery.

"A key goal of continuous delivery is to change the economics of the software delivery process to make it economically viable to work in small batches so we can obtain the many benefits of this approach."
- Jez Humble[37]

I couldn't have phrased it any better! For that we need to also make decisions in smaller batches, so that it can be out sooner and economically viable. Our story is a perfect example of what I see way too often: teams can go fast, *real fast*! But if the rest of the organisation doesn't keep up, it defeats the object.

Delivering value early and constantly should also account for packaging, legacy systems you may have as it's not always about starting from scratch and also comprises things that may not be necessarily software. Either way, small feedback loops are key as an enabler.

Also, I want to highlight the importance of using automated version control[38] which ensures that nothing important is lost when changes are made to a collaborative project. Development branches are to have a small and short shelf life, items continuously integrated and each change is to trigger a build

37   Jez Humble, "Principles", Continuous Delivery, https://continuousdelivery.com/principles/

38   Ines Garcia, "Salesforce Git for Admins", Quality Clouds, https://www.qualityclouds.com/salesforce-git-for-admins/

process that includes running tests, so if anything fails this is made known and gets fixed right there and then.

Feedback[39] is one of the values of Extreme Programming, and has a few dimensions: feedback from the system for example as monitoring and regular integration tests, feedback from the users which should steer the direction of the development and feedback from the team.

The concept of shifting left[40] (the idea of incorporating feedback and testing way early and throughout the development cycle) supports feedback and integrates assurance, confidence and trust in the product. Automatically and continuously, also being notified right away if something is not as expected, bringing the concept of monitoring not just for usage but for performance.

---

39   "Extreme Programming", Wikipedia, https://en.wiki-pedia.org/wiki/Extreme_programming#Values

40   "Shift Left Testing", Wikipedia, https://en.wikipedia.org/wiki/Shift-left_testing.

Tip

Looking back at the story, I'm sure there were many things that could have been done to convey that agreement with the rest of the organisation that the Product Owner found quite challenging. I'll give you one tip that I don't see often enough and that from my experience seems to work quite well:

Show the product, show it often and show it to all!

Because the nature of our work is creative, we invent things, showing how the concepts are translated into the product is very powerful. So at the end of every week, gather with the team and interested parties such as the sponsors, other teams, end users… and show them: This is what we discussed to do, this is how it looks and performs.

In Scrum, which I define as a lightweight framework to get into an agile rhythm, one of the touch points in every iteration is what's called the Sprint Review. By 'touch points' I mean the moments in every cycle where we come together at the same time, in the same place and for the same reasons.

"A Sprint Review is held at the end of the Sprint to inspect the Increment and adapt the Product Backlog if needed. During the Sprint Review, the Scrum Team and stakeholders collaborate

about what was done in the Sprint. [...] This is an informal meeting, not a status meeting, and the presentation of the Increment is intended to elicit feedback and foster collaboration. "[41]

The *Sprint* is a cycle or iteration of product delivery. If then in the Sprint Review the Product Owner does the *show and tell* and runs the demo, that's even better!

With this simple exercise, which shouldn't be too lengthy (start short and sweet), you are essentially opening up a space for collaboration to refine your understanding of where you are going.

It also really helps to imagine and *slice* (remember page 42) the product increments into manageable pieces of work, so that it can actually be shown by the end of the week.

---

41 "The Scrum Guide", Scrum Guides, https://www. scrumguides.org/scrum-guide.html#events-review

Why not try...

Demo often to ALL by ALL.

Make an open, 30-minute calendar recurrence. Make it visible and open to all in the organisation, attendance is completely optional.

There you will show your latest increment on what you've been working towards. To start you can even get a couple more teams on board and rotate who shows their recent development in which week.

Compress the presentation into 15 minutes and allow the other fifteen for questions, ideas and general praise.

This acts as a good reminder for where we are headed together so that the whole organisation can align, be transparent, and naturally tune and adjust from other inputs.

It also provides a much-needed time for acknowledging what's going well and who's making what happen: a moment of recognition that makes people happy. Who likes doing a good job and getting thanks for it?

And don't you worry if not many people attend, ultimately you are inviting the whole organisation so everyone has to find balance and make their own judgement based on what else they have on their plate at the time. You are making it possible for people to attend and that's what matters, and that's an extremely valuable exercise for the team in itself.

As with all experiments it is up to us to practise what we preach, again, we have to start with ourselves. You can't ask others to behave differently if you don't. Improve yourself first.

Treat things to try as experiments, experiments being things that you learn from and tweak as you go forward.

Semantics

You may encounter some resistance from many angles here: how to slice the ideas, how it can be built smaller, how to slice the work so that it can be shown sooner, how it can be demoed every week, how can 'we' attend every week...

To whomever is expressing that resistance, please explain briefly the intention of the benefits from the exercise, then add, "Are you willing to give it a try?" Who says no to that?!

Also to note beyond semantics check out the article on the notes here about slicing and simplification[42] for some ideas.

---

42   "A #NoEstimates tool: The slicing meeting, replacing estimation meetings while creating shared understanding", Software Development Today, http://softwaredevelopmenttoday. com/2017/10/a-noestimates-tool-the-slicing-meeting-replacing-estimation-meetings-while-creating-shared-understanding/

Book

User Stories Applied - Mike Cohn[43]

To me, this book is great for getting into the nitty-gritty of how to slice up the work so that you can then deliver value early and continuously. It also covers how to organise and prioritise that sliced work, including for planning and testing.

By defining the breakdown of work and defining its purpose; the 'why', rather than the 'how' it will be done. As Product Owner, trust your team. They solve much harder problems every day and they definitely have the know-how.

---

43   Mike Cohn, *User Stories Applied*, (Boston: Pearson Education, Inc., 2004)

Welcome Change whilst there is Return On Investment

"Welcome changing requirements, even late in development. Agile processes harness change for the customer's competitive advantage."
- Agile Manifesto[44]

---

44   Mike Beedle et al., "The Agile Manifesto", Agile Manifesto, 2001, https://agilemanifesto.org

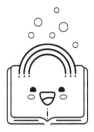

Don't Bite Off More than You Can Chew

Sai, Ashley and Zane ordered in some pizza and prepared for another long night.

As a Salesforce team with email marketing experience they'd been really looking forward to working together on their main goal, which was building scalable solutions for digital marketing automation.

They'd started by taking on board some simple email sends to get the structure of data sets and assets ready, and also to act as a bit of a safety net for the communications team in the early days of the tool implementation.

Over time what actually happened was that the team found themselves doing a lot of one-off tasks and business-as-usual activities. Technology updates weren't able to be implemented as fast as had been hoped. The plan to architect a self-service tool so that the organisation could deliver value sooner whilst getting the most return from their investment was also falling victim to these mundane and relentless tasks.

Hence the pizza. They were a committed team who really cared about doing a good job, saying yes and making things happen. As time in the working day was eaten up with the quotidien jobs they found themselves working evenings and weekends to manually push email sends. Why? Perhaps it was due to uncertainty about the application, maybe a shortage of trust in the scheduling functionality, or nervousness surrounding the lack of refactoring...

Into this busy and frustrated team came yet another job. It was presented as an idea in rough terms and with an insanely short deadline. This rough idea was about an email weekly recurrence to encourage all subscribers to increase their engagement with the brand.

"The necessary refactoring hasn't been done, and I don't know who we can talk to about this. My family are already getting tetchy about the amount of hours I'm working and this means we'll be generating a number of separate emails, with separate structures, separate assets, separate segmentations and exclusions every week! And none of it's even reusable!" Sai was getting really stressed.

"You're right, Sai. This is so fiddly it's going to take at least 15% of all our capacity," agreed Zane.

"There isn't 15% left when we're already working at 100," Ashley pointed out.

Nevertheless, the team ploughed on. At a cost. More hours, less rest, more shortcuts, less headspace, more intensity... more burden.

It's not only a mathematical impossibility to work at 115% of capacity, it's also thoroughly undesirable to even attempt it, for many reasons, as the team were discovering. Other tasks were getting neglected and their wellbeing was taking a huge hit. They sucked it up and kept trying because that's the kind of people they were.

They tried to engage the extended leadership team about the situation and a few failed conversations were had. Eventually, Maria, one of the members of the senior leadership team, asked, "but what is the return of investment on this thing?" That forced a pause. They looked at some reports, dug into the data, tried to validate their efforts. The outcome of that exercise was that so far the effort didn't provide any argument to further pursue the 'rough' idea that had come from nowhere.

There are many things to be untangled from this story, some of which I will cover later on in the following chapters. I felt for the team and I felt for the application! But let's stick to the concept at hand:

Welcome Change whilst there is Return On Investment.

In the last chapter we uncovered the concept of sizing, all ideas are ultimately bets: *"Risk something, usually a sum of money, against someone else's on the basis of the outcome of a future event, such as the result of a race or game."*[45]

I shall then say that a business idea is a risk of value (time, effort, intelligence and money) against other competitors' on the basis of the outcome of an unpredictable market and ever changing environment.

And bets, ideas, tries, experiments… When these flourish, that's what makes the difference. It's what keeps the organisation afloat, what gives you an advantage over other brands and what, ultimately, brings the return on investment.

But don't risk it all and don't risk it blindly.

---

45   'Bet', Lexico, https://www.lexico.com/en/definition/bet

"Just because something has been a lot of work or consumed a lot of time doesn't make it productive or worthwhile" - Tim Ferris[46]

Openness plays a vital part here. It is one of the Scrum values and included in this idea is two-way openness: with and from the interested parties (such as the stakeholders). This covers agreeing with each other to all be open about the work and about the challenges of performing it: what is stopping or slowing us down? What are the difficulties and what is *not* bringing us closer to the common goal?

---

46   Tim Ferris, "Killing Your Job", Fast Company, 19/January/11, https://www.fastcompany.com/1718578/killing-your-job

Tip

Like with diet and exercise there is a tipping point where over time, less benefit is derived from each extra unit of time/effort invested. In economics, they call this 'the law of diminishing returns'[47]. To be able to continue trading beyond the right now it's important to watch this tipping point carefully across the different things we have in motion, so that we can help ourselves and reduce waste by recognising it and diverting the time and effort elsewhere.

In this story we could be talking about the importance of tradeoffs for new effort that landed in the team's work tray, or about catching it earlier before it had got there, or many other things that surely you have seen and thought about. I, however, would like to give you a different perspective.

In the last chapter we talked about the importance of showing the product: the more feedback loops you have, the more ideas will emerge. It's natural and it's a good thing.

47   "Diminishing returns", Wikipedia, https://en.wikipedia.org/wiki/Diminishing_returns

Slicing ideas into smaller ones - which I like to call 'bets' - allows easier experimentation so that the hypothesis can either be pursued or discontinued.

Now let's focus more on the granular level of time allocated for a task; look at your day-to-day as an example.

"Work expands so as to fill the time available for its completion" - Parkinson's law[48]

The more time we ringfence to do something, the more time we will invest doing the thing. Parkinson's Law refers to the growth of bureaucracy in an organisation. You can apply it to a team and its environment as the operating system that it is.

So, finally, my tip for this chapter is to ringfence time. A common term in Agile jargon is 'timeboxing', which originated in project management (especially lean project management).

You can timebox changes, timebox experiments and timebox investigations (often referred to as *spikes*[49]) so that it has minimal impact on everything else.

It comes especially handy as changes are not like-for-like, it already has an extra weight for the context switch and let's not forget about the time already invested in the initial thought path that will no longer be valid. Within those timeboxes stay away from interfering and distracting teams, and help others including team members to do so themselves.

Welcome change whilst there is return or a strong hypothesis of a higher return than not doing so, so what you can test on a small, ringfenced effort so that you can faster validate or revoke your hypothesis.

---

48   "Parkinson's law", Wikipedia, https://en.wikipedia.org/wiki/Parkinson%27s_law

49   Spikes help us to understand more, whether that's product, solution, technology, options, etc. The term is most often used in agile software development approaches to explore ways to reduce uncertainty. The term originated from Extreme Programming.

And yes, this even applies to late development, since there's no point in delivering something that won't be fit for purpose. Change is part of nature and we need to become more comfortable with allowing it in when there is value.

"Passion is the bridge that takes you from pain to change" - Frida Kahlo[50]

Talking about being comfortable with change and in the context of email marketing from our chapter story, one of the dangers of being uncomfortable with change and that negatively affects one's business is the fallacy of not-letting-go. Organisations that keep sending blast emails which are not targeted, not personalised, not tested at small scale with control groups, not letting go (data deletion) of subscribers which are not engaged with the brand, etc. All of which has a direct detrimental effect to one's domain reputation and also to your brand[51].

---

50   Frida Kahlo, "Frida Kahlo Quote", AZ Quotes, https://www.azquotes.com/quote/811637

51   "Email Deliverability Review", Data & Marketing Association,   https://dma.org.uk/uploads/Email%20Deliverability%20-%20Whitepaper_53cf9dddc9c03.pdf

Why not try...

Before you go gung ho and timebox everything, let's start small, with yourself. For the following days, timebox in your calendar some of the things you want to accomplish, perhaps even start with the ones you've been postponing for a while.

The trick here is to be fair to yourself by:

- Making your goals realistic, and
- Sticking with it

How do you think I ended up writing this book?

One of the things that is key to this is to enable a state of flow, a state of deep thinking, a full-on concentration state. That takes around 15-20 minutes to get into, it's like an inmersion, so consider this when you schedule timeboxing.

Also a disruptive work environment, not only noise but your workspace, including digital distractions which are a killer; once the state of flow is broken by interruption the brain needs to go back again to step one of immersion[52].

---

52   'Mental State Called Flow', Wiki, https://wiki.c2.com/?-MentalStateCalledFlow

What seems to work quite well for me is to add some bullet points and train of thought when I book a timebox in the calendar. So that when it gets to that time, the effort of context switching reduces.

Semantics

You may already have spotted it whilst reading this chapter, I have continuously used words like *bets*. This helps to reinforce the uncertainty of the *what*, the *how* and the *when* of the things at hand. You may want to add to your list of words: ideas, hypothesis, about, approximate, roughly, guess...

I'd also suggest avoiding the word *risk*, it has quite a negative connotation and is often abused in a more traditional way of project delivery. On the spot you most likely won't have an audience with enough headspace and willingness to hear the context, so it is best just to avoid it. In addition with any risk comes an opportunity, we often rarely consider them and so by using the word bet, this gives the connotation that there is a potential win.

Book

Improv-Ing Agile Teams: Using Constraints to Unlock Creativity - Paul Goddard[53]

We humans improvise everyday, constantly. This book is one of a kind, it brings a bunch of improv (acting) techniques to teamwork covering key areas such as safety, spontaneity and storytelling. And how using constraints one can unlock creativity.

---

53   Paul Goddard, *Improv-Ing Agile Teams*, (Bradford on Avon: Agilify, 2015)

Deliver Working Product Frequently

"Deliver working software frequently, from a couple of weeks to a couple of months, with a preference to the shorter timescale." - Agile Manifesto[54]

---

54   Jim Highsmith, "The Agile Manifesto", Agile Manifesto, 2001, https://agilemanifesto.org

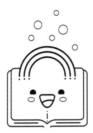

Actions Speak Louder Than Words

It was mid-January and the Christmas cheer was wearing off. What the team needed was a new project. So when they were given eight weeks to produce a proof of concept for a chatbot they were pumped to get started.

Akari explained the task to the rest of the team. "A proof of concept is like a prototype. It is often small and possibly incomplete, but exists to demonstrate a working product, idea, method, technology, etc. Our challenge is to put together the proof of concept in eight weeks and reach a point where a working chatbot can be demonstrated."

Chatbots are becoming more and more common - you've probably come across more than one - and are where a software application is used to initiate and then conduct an on-line text conversation with a customer, meaning a webchat with an agent isn't necessary unless requested.

The team were super excited about this challenge. "Salesforce offers an extension of the web chat capability which we already have in place to do exactly what we need!" pointed out Ric, enthusiastically. "We can harness the elasticity in that technology to deliver faster at scale and id push boundaries through constant innovation." Choosing tools, technology and partners which enabled them to grow and flourish and which complemented their goals and offered room for growth meant that all they could see in planning to develop this proof of concept was opportunities and choices rather than obstacles and dead ends.

Akari was leading the initial meeting and explaining the plan. "OK, let's start by analysing contact trends to explore why customers are making contact in the first place. If there are scenarios which keep coming up then they'll be prime candidates for automation."

Once they'd found high-volume web transactions, they prioritised them by considering:

- size (how much effort will it take)

- anticipated return on investment (how many conversations will be diverted from humans to the chatbot)

- complexity (how sure are we about the reasons for these contacts)

- how to avoid time-hungry and complex authentication scenarios

So they started small. Their first chatbot gave a simple list of options to triage work and route it to the appropriate queue. Omnichannel[55], a functionality they were already using, then prompted service agents with availability and the right skills to handle the incoming chat.

Ric, the Salesforce guru, suggested the next iteration goal. "Let's extend the list of options available to the

---

55   "Omni-Channel", Salesforce, https://help.salesforce.com/articleView?id=omnichannel_intro.htm&type=5

customer to include the facility to remind them of their delivery date. All that information is already in Salesforce, all we have to do is ask the customer their order number as input, then display back into the chatbot the expected delivery date value field. There would be zero customer or privacy data retrieved or disclosed. It's a no-brainer!"

Week after week, an improvement or extension was added. So by the end of the first quarter, not only did they have that proof of concept but they had three chatbots deployed and functioning in a live environment!

And that's a story I very much enjoy sharing!

The improvements and extensions kept on coming. Even not long after the team added the ability for the chatbot to surface relevant knowledge articles within the chat (that's made easier thanks to a feature added by a recent Salesforce release).

As you probably know, Salesforce as a technology provider enhances their offering constantly that includes three major releases a year, where tonnes of new features are distributed across the entire customer portfolio with no downtime. Some are new paid add-ons but most are just free and ready for you to use. To me, taking advantage of these is getting the most return of investment in your contract with Salesforce.

Going back to the principle at hand here, in our story to enable the three chatbots to go out the door in a short timescale was only possible with ruthless prioritization and sizing. By sizing I mean how it is you slice the effort that accounts for an end to end piece of product, which includes three layers: business logic, database and user interface. The way that you size is key so that by every end of iteration you have a potentially shippable product.

That means a fully finished product, not 90% done but done-done. A potentially shippable product. So it's a case of just pressing a button and having it deployed, a working product, in the market, in the hands of end users. Every single end of iteration.

Here is where the Definition of Done[56] comes to play. Having a clear and tangible definition of what classifies a sprint-committed item as done drives the quality of work and is used to assess when a user story has been completed. It's for the team to define their Definition of Done to achieve alignment among themselves, thus enabling a clear idea of what will define a 'piece of work' as being done, ensuring that everyone on the team knows exactly what is expected of each bit the team delivers. It may start something like this:

- Meets acceptance criteria set by Product Owner
- Peer reviewed
- In line with approved industry & company standards
- The work is briefly documented as part of budget job allocation
- Showed/demoed to customer
- Joins with existing parts (Incremental)
- Allows consolidation of upcoming parts (Iterative)

That definition is kept alive; it is presented at the start of every iteration, revised, and agreement is reached if any change is to be made. As the team matures, the Definition of Done expands to include more strict criteria and evolves further over time.

As a team you may want to use visuals to display that end to end / done-done, to be able to visualise your workflow.

"Our goal is to make deployments—whether of a large-scale distributed system, a complex production environment, an embedded system, or an app—predictable, routine affairs that can be performed on demand.

---

56   "The Scrum Guide", Scrum Guides, https://www. scrumguides.org/scrum-guide.html#artifact-transparency-done

We achieve all this by ensuring our code is always in a deployable state, even in the face of teams of thousands of developers making changes on a daily basis. We thus completely eliminate the integration, testing and hardening phases that traditionally followed "dev complete", as well as code freezes."- Jez Humble, Continuous Delivery[57]

I did say *potentially* shippable product, as at times for example the Product Owner may decide to wait another iteration to have the product within the customers' hands to get the most of return or to coordinate for training the end users if the new functionality coming in really requires that.

"*The basic idea of separating deployments from releases is to hide work from end users, either because it's not ready for them or because they're not ready for it*" - Andrew Davis, Mastering Salesforce DevOps[58]

Frequent Delivery is a common property from the Crystal family[59]. That regular releasing through iterations enables the team, including Product Owner, to spot issues and to gather feedback to inform next steps.

---

57   Jez Humble, "What is Continuous Delivery?", Continuous Delivery, https://continuousdelivery.com

58   Andrew Davis, *Mastering Salesforce DevOps: A Practical Guide to Building Trust While Delivering Innovation,* (San Diego: Apress, 2019), https://www.amazon.com/Andrew-Davis/e/B07Y-7QC8WF

59   "Crystal Methods", Wikiversity, https://en.wikiversity.org/wiki/Crystal_Methods

Tip

I have mentioned iterations and cycles, that in 'Agile jargon' is often called a Sprint[60]. This is the biggest timebox you have as a small cycle of product delivery. Within it you do few things like the Sprint Review we mentioned earlier, to show your product often and to gain continuous feedback.

In the Scrum guide, where the Scrum framework is based, a sprint is defined with length of up to one month or less with preferences for a smaller time frame. For what I have seen the most often used is a sprint length of two weeks. But it is really for the team to decide, if you deploy nowadays every three months, then moving into maybe two weeks is a good experiment to try. Remember back on *page 58*, when we saw that Parkinson's Law says that work expands in the time given?

Although my tip here is that if you are new to all of this, then set your delivery cycles as something you and everybody else have in place and are familiar with, a timebox that gives us a rhythm in our day to day life:

Try your sprint length of a week.

---

60   "The Scrum Guide", Scrum Guides, https://www. scrumguides.org/scrum-guide.html#events-sprint

Most of us are already used to starting the week on Monday morning and having to switch on to what we are to tackle for the week ahead, to get to Friday to finish up some things before the weekend. Please try it, it will feel so much more natural than any other time frame.

In addition, it's easier to assess what can be done in five days. A week, that's your bigger timebox to deliver potentially shippable product increment towards your team's common goal.

At the start of the week discuss what can realistically be done in that week and refine a bit how to tackle it with your team. Then every day tune and adjust towards that common goal that you have committed as a team at the start of the week. Then at the end of your week show it to all, get feedback to inform your next steps and enjoy the weekend!

In addition, sprints bring you two more things. Small wins and fresh starts both translate into boosts of energy and morale.

Why not try...

Things evolve and new ideas will emerge and that's a good thing! Because of it there is always a need to triage them so that they can be placed (or not) in the already existing priority list.

There are few techniques for these kinds of situations, I'd like to introduce to you the Eisenhower Matrix[61] to give it a try.

The Eisenhower Matrix is composed of a quadrant of urgency and importance, separated into four sections:

61   Development That Pays, "The Eisenhower Matrix - aka The Time Management Matrix", YouTube, 4/February/18, https://www.youtube.com/watch?v=DX4LStJGny4

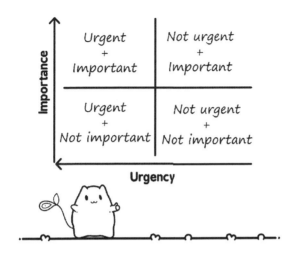

If you have read the book *The 7 Habits of Highly Effective People* by Stephen R. Covey[62] this will ring a bell, as his time management matrix was based on this.

Looking at the quadrants the idea is to triage the things in the simplest possible way:

---

62   Stephen R. Covey, The 7 Habits of Highly Effective People, (London: Simon & Schuster UK Ltd, 1989)

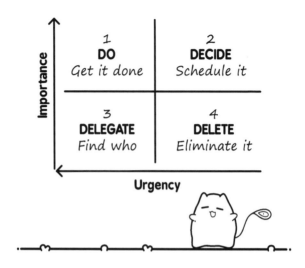

The YouTube video added here in the notes[63] is great to complement this concept. And absolutely yes to the fourth quadrant, just don't do it!

If you can actually have it scribbled somewhere, that's even better, thanks to the power of the visuals this will surface the new idea coming in against the other things in motion, it's easier to compare. It's a relative exercise rather than absolute, more informed and within context.

---

63   Development That Pays, "The Eisenhower Matrix - aka The Time Management Matrix", YouTube, 4/February/18, https://www.youtube.com/watch?v=DX4LStJGny4

Semantics

Avoid the word *requirement*, it's defined by Google as '*a thing that is needed or wanted*'. It seems to me that people only read as far as the '*needed*' as if it were a matter of survival.

This word just comes with so much baggage, when just over 100 years ago it barely existed:

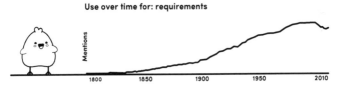

Use over time for: requirements

64

Instead what you want to reinforce is the goal of the effort. Describe a product feature from an end-user perspective, what they want, why and the reasoning behind it. The move to context and logic instead of a dictated to-do list. People think in narratives, user stories enable just that.

You would still have some specifications around the look and feel, load speed, reusability etc. but that would be with any-

---

64   "Requirements", Google Books Ngram Viewer, http://tiny.cc/requirement

thing coming up for the application at hand. These things are worth considering as part of your team's definition of done, a definition which is alive and is to evolve over time.

Book

The 7 Habits of Highly Effective People - Stephen R. Covey[65]

You may have guessed my book recommendation while reading the experiment on this chapter.

This book is more than just some tools like the time management quadrant, it is an introspection journey to oneself and the world around us, it gives you a High Definition lens about behavioural patterns and their reasoning, starting with your own.

65   Stephen R. Covey, *The 7 Habits of Highly Effective People,* (London: Simon & Schuster UK Ltd, 1989)

Forget about the 'Them' and 'Us'

"Business people and developers must work together daily through-out the project." - Agile Manifesto[66]

---

66   Jim Highsmith, "History: The Agile Manifesto", Agile Manifesto, 2001, https://agilemanifesto.org/history.html

If You Want to Go Far, Go Together

Picture the scene… A virtual assistant startup is deciding what CRM software to use. They decide upon Salesforce and use that to track all their operations.

Over time, the business grows. Within this expansion they create different member tiers and support 24/7 operations in multiple languages across multiple locations.

They have a system which works. The team leader on shift, with the help of some of the more experienced team members, triages the cases and chats coming in and allocates them accordingly to virtual assistants. This circuitous process has been put in place by the operations team with the intention of avoiding cherry-picking and increasing efficiency. The consequence in reality is that they are starting to compromise the speed, which is resulting in some challenges from customers.

It has become clear that their systems need a rethink.

The team looking after the Salesforce application therefore have a new challenge; Casey, the Salesforce Administrator, Kwame, the Business Analyst and Elena, a

Salesforce Developer are given the job of automating the work coming in so that there is no need for team leaders to triage and allocate. They already have in place live chat, web-to-case[67] and email-to-case[68] functionality.

After a bit of googling[69], the Salesforce team consider a few ideas and decide to investigate further OmniChannel[70], an out-of-the-box functionality[71]. OmniChannel is already included in the contract of Service Cloud licences, so there is no further cost, and an out-of-the-box functionality means that it's supported, extended and upgraded in every Salesforce major release.

The investigation becomes a proof of concept for live chats by language, so that when a new chat comes in it is already allocated to a specific queue where the agents are assigned in such a way as to ensure that they are served the correct type of work.

The Salesforce team show their progress and concept to Deepa, the Head of Operations. The feedback is excellent and the fast turnaround so impressive that the

67   Web-to-case: functionality which lets your customers submit support requests on your website creating a servicing support record in your Salesforce CRM.

68   Email-to-case: Salesforce automatically creates cases and auto-populates case fields when customers send messages to the email addresses you specify.

69   Googling, which we all do, is the act of searching for information about someone or something on the Internet using the search engine Google.

70   "Omni-Channel for Administrators", Salesforce, https://help.salesforce.com/articleView?id=service_presence_intro.htm&type=5

71   Out-of-the-box: a feature or functionality of a product that works without any special installation without any modification; it's ready to go.

Salesforce team are asked then to schedule the work to go live the following week.

Our team are buoyed with enthusiasm. They have risen to all the challenges that growth has thrown their way. They have exploited the functionality of the software they already have and identified new tools to meet their ongoing needs. They have managed all this in a way that not only pleases Deepa but also gets the job done in a way which achieves all their goals.

Imagine their surprise when, the next day, the Resource Manager storms in to their office ranting that the new functionality will never work. Announcing that, "They don't want it! They won't use it! They aren't ready! They don't like it!"

But, "They…"

Who are "they"?!

One of the interesting things is that, more often than not, the "they" tends to be hierarchical. One or more people in a team don't believe the team can proceed with their best knowledge and intention for a greater good. This seems to me like a self-imposed limitation.

It comes as a version of appearance of being trapped by a system, for example; "That it was already decided". It's just like being in an operating system prison.

The entity of 'them/they' may often take the form of 'The Business', as though there is an imagined body higher up the ladder of bureaucracy that has already decided that anything you try won't work. Remember 'them' is an imaginary entity. You are not trapped in a system.

Yet there's another way to interpret this story. It talks to us about a 'boss' creating resistance from preconceptions of their own team, and that's without even seeing the proposed functionality.

I ask the teams I work with (annoyingly or not) when this 'mysterious entity' appears in conversation, "who are they?". I find it frustrating, 'yet at the same time quite amusing' that we, humans, have created this entity of 'them/they' that rule above us.

We must also acknowledge from this story that there are lots of reactions driven from impulse rather than a conscious decision. Such as the decision of the Resource Manager (don't get me started on the job title) reacting by storming into a team's working area to make a physical statement and causing a kerfuffle.

Not only is that negative, disruptive and selfish; such reactions are founded by something, most likely fear. For example: a fear of the unknown or fear of losing control, which could potentially have been the triggers here. Understandably, as humans in our nature we crave the need to control. Whether that's controlling ourselves or controlling others around us[72].

Through the practice of 'showing the product and showing it to all', the team is able to create a space to:

- explain what they were trying to achieve and the challenge given

- show the actual features and show it within context

- clarify any questions

- receive valuable feedback from the consumers/end users.

Constant seeking for anything that enhances communication. Another of the Extreme Programming (XP) values: **Communication**[73], and this can take many forms, and yes it will

---

72   Timothy Carey, "The Being of Humans", Psychology Today, 9/October/15, https://www.psychologytoday.com/gb/blog/in-control/201510/the-being-humans

73   "Extreme Programming", Wikipedia, https://en.wikipedia.org/wiki/Extreme_programming#Values

include documentation as we have already covered, frequent feedback as we also covered and verbal communication. So that end users, consumers, development teams and the rest of the organisation have a shared understanding and view of the product. Some of the XP techniques support exactly that, a fast generation and spread of institutional knowledge. Think about communication as an easy access to expert users of which we learn from Crystal[74], and therefore fading the lines between 'them/they' and 'us'.

---

74   "Crystal Methods", Wikiversity, https://en.wikiversity. org/wiki/Crystal_Methods

Tip

We have already touched on this tip, but I urge you to join me in addressing the amusingly annoying *imagined entity*. When hearing, "They want this," "They want it sooner," or, "They said no…" just ask, "Who are they?"

To combat self-imposed limitations you may want to ask, "Why don't we just ask? What's the worst that can happen?" Once that first barrier of resistance is down and you go and speak with 'them', then ask a ton of questions. There is where the value lies, in the narrative, the individual and the interactions, working together towards the common goal.

Firstly by understanding where the train of thought initially came from, this then aids an understanding of the context and reasoning of resistance. The question, "Who are they?" reverts back the conversation of purpose, therefore finding out the motivation, a reason or reasons for acting or behaving in a particular way.

Listening with the intent to understand, to understand others' points of view. And treating each other as humans, not a cluster entity.

To deepen our understanding of the 'entity' in question, it also helps to use real people's names instead as we are all individuals, not an amalgamation of evil entities called 'them'. Using people's names builds a sense of familiarity, it brings the matter at hand closer and reduces the unconscious guard that many times we humans build up.

This reminds me of The Prime Directive:

"Regardless of what we discover, we understand and truly believe that everyone did the best job they could, given what they knew at the time, their skills and abilities, the resources available, and the situation at hand." - Norm Kerth, Project Retrospectives[75]

Although the above is most often used around team retrospectives[76] (a concept we will touch on later), it's a powerful concept and useful to remind oneself of. We as people get stuck on our own ideas when the reality doesn't match that, we don't always take it very well.

"Be less curious about people and more curious about ideas" - Marie Curie[77]

---

75   "The Prime Directive", Retrospective Wiki, https://retrospectivewiki.org/index.php?title=The_Prime_Directive

76   "What is a Sprint Retrospective?", Scrum, https://www.scrum.org/resources/what-is-a-sprint-retrospective

77   Marie Curie, "Marie Curie", Wikiquote, https://en.wikiquote.org/wiki/Marie_Curie

Why not try...

The work that we do is related to users, teams, end consumers, other technologies… you name it. An interconnecting network.

That interconnecting network is a system and, as any system, after a certain size and volume it can have a detrimental effect. Hence the concepts of modular architecture, packaging, asynchronicity...

Because an organisation is an operating system in itself, it requires quality of interactions to perform at its best.

These quality interactions span across all exchanges between the different containers such as projects, teams, products, organisations etc. as loosely-coupled architecture. And fostering that diversity in each container to accelerate and enrich the product.

Encourage and enable diverse teams with a common goal, so that people can stimulate and learn from each other, with a varied and rich background, training, skills, etc. we must make a conscious effort to amplify and build upon each other's ideas.

The Organisation System Architecture topic deserves its own book. But for now let's call the experiment of this chapter: cross-functional grouplets[78].

Generally in organisations we tend to group ourselves by the technology that we use rather than the value that we bring. The unintended outcome of doing so is an increase of cycle time[79], that translates to the day-to-day in waiting for other teams to provide X or finish with Y, so that another team can start Z.

Map out the current themes of work you have in play, visualise the interconnections with other teams and how often those happen. Notice as well if there is any theme that needs more of an input on the day-to-day for delivery that you may have not realised.

As usual, start small and start experimentally. An example of a great grouplet that I have seen performing in the Salesforce world had skills of Salesforce development, marketing/campaign management, Marketing Cloud[80] development, quality assurance and commercial. Together, day in day out working towards their common goal.

Suggest giving it a try! Observe if that eases and speeds up delivery with less waiting time and fewer interruptions.

---

78 "A "grouplet": a small, self-organized team that has almost no budget and even less authority, but that tries to change something within the company." Daniel H. Pink, Drive: The Surprising Truth About What Motivates Us, (Edinburgh: Canongate Books Ltd., 2018)

79 "Cycle Time", Wiktionary, https://en.wiktionary.org/wiki/cycle_time

80 "Marketing Cloud is a digital marketing platform from Salesforce which includes tools for email marketing, social media marketing, mobile marketing, online advertising, and marketing automation." "Marketing Cloud Overview", Salesforce, https://www.salesforce.com/uk/products/marketing-cloud/overview/

Semantics

Avoid giving the usual labels for your grouplet. Words such as *squad*, *project team*, *Scrum team*, *delivery team*, maybe just *team*? These labels come with way too much baggage, to what individuals have experienced, read or through hearsay.

No one really needs to know what you are doing, just find a way to group together on a daily basis towards a weekly goal, and ask, "Do we have the skills that we need?"

Book

Collective Genius: The Art and Practice of Leading Innovation - Linda A. Hill et al[81]

This book is based on research of various organisations where innovation seems part of their DNA. It takes you through a series of stories highlighting commonalities between the organisations of research, and you will gather tons of ideas for how to enable an environment that stimulates innovation.

---

81   Linda A. Hill et al., *Collective Genius: The Art and Practice of Leading Innovation*, (Boston: Harvard Business Review, 2014)

Supercharge with Motivation

"Build projects around motivated individuals. Give them the environment and support they need, and trust them to get the job done." - Agile Manifesto[82]

82   Jim Highsmith, "History: The Agile Manifesto", Agile Manifesto, 2001, https://agilemanifesto.org/history.html

Standing on Thin Ice

Enrique's chair was empty. He had been called away by a personal emergency and was unable to give a return date. The team who looked after and extended the Salesforce organisation would be a man down for the foreseeable future.

The rest of the team managed to hold the fort for the next few weeks, getting all business-as-usual activities completed. Dan, who had several years of experience, was promoted despite only recently having joined the company.

The following months brought quite a few last minute emergencies, specifically partner contractual agreements with fixed scope, fixed delivery dates and all agreed without involving the team.

"Has anyone else noticed that there seems to be a trend developing?" asked Lou. "We're only getting passed commercial agreements days before the signed go live date. It feels like we're working really long days just to develop quick 'tactical' solutions and workarounds so we can get them out of the door. It just doesn't feel quite like what we're here for."

There was general agreement around the office; they were spending more and more time working reactively, rather than proactively or creatively.

Another layer of disruption was added when, a couple of months later, the Head of the Department announced that she was leaving. She was acknowledged and respected as someone who insulated the team from unnecessary distractions, politics and burden, and her absence was going to be felt.

Without her to absorb and deflect, the last minute emergencies flung at the team increased, and the demands made of them from elsewhere in the business ratcheted up.

"You have to change something. The team can't continue this way," Lou pleaded with the senior leaders. "Not only is it an unhealthy way of working but it's also bad practice in terms of the architecture and scalability of our Salesforce platform. These quick 'tactical' solutions we are being forced to implement have knock-on effects to the customer services team who in turn have to live with increased workarounds in their day-to-day job, with the potential for things to take longer and have a greater margin of error. The situation is bad for us as humans and it's also bad for business."

But nothing was done to try to find a solution. The problems continued to grow over the next few weeks and a new habit was born. An unacceptable habit. A habit where people from other teams started barging in to their working space. "Just get it done!" "I need this right now!" "Make it happen!" Such demands became a soundtrack to their working day. Shouting matches were not unheard of and storming off became an uncomfortably regular occurrence.

The rest of the organisation had very little empathy for the team. No one seemed to care that, in these abnormal circumstances, they needed time to adjust to the loss of two team members and to work out how to ramp up their skills to fulfil the responsibilities which these two roles had met.

You won't be surprised to learn that every couple of weeks someone handed their notice in. People had had enough. This exodus wasn't confined to the Salesforce team; members of other teams working closely with them also started leaving the company.

No wonder. The team had no autonomy over their work, they had no headspace nor time for self or team improvement and the work they were doing was not scalable. The road down which the team had been forced was a one which slowly but surely stripped them of their purpose. With directives like 'do this', 'do it now', and 'do it like this', who actually needed them?

This story is basically the opposite of what we need in our operating system environment. The above is a sum of what really defeats the concept of *quality of interactions*.

Based on extensive research about behaviour, the surprising truth of what motivates us is intrinsic, it comes from within. It's based on having autonomy in the work that we do, on mastery (the need to get better at what we do) and on contributing to a purpose larger than ourselves. Some of you may have seen the Dan Pink whiteboard version of his TED talk on the subject.[83] And in our story this team had none of it.

Another milder version of defeating interactions which I notice often is what I call the 'no no no' hat. Remember a situation

---

83   The RSAy, "RSA ANIMATE: Drive: The surprising truth about what motivates us", YouTube, 1/April/10, https://www.youtube.com/watch?v=u6XAPnuFjJc

when you were proposing an idea or an alternative and all you got back was a 'no'? That's what I'm talking about.

We need to get out of the 'discomfort zone' of new ideas, get rid of that barrier of resistance we generate about the unknown. Especially as the work that we do is not about recreation, but creation. Creative thinking, after all, is hard. It requires right-brain thinking, the capacity to have time to think and the ability to be flexible enough to problem solve.

Different ideas are just that: another outlook on the same situation. We saw earlier (Page: 88) that understanding the context, gathering knowledge and doing it collaboratively helps to form better informed options to decide from.

Moving away from the fear of conflict, understanding that constructive disagreement can help us. Conflict, when healthy, can be useful for leading to better decisions, better ways, better ideas, better performance and better products. All round better-ness.

The importance of **Personal Safety**, another common property that we learn from the Crystal family[84]. The people in the team must be able to trust each other, feel free and compelled to speak up about issues or whatever arises, knowing that they will be supported.

"When turning a group of strangers into a team, look for how quickly you can find the unique talents, skills and hopes of each person, and how quickly you can convey what you bring." - Amy Edmondson[85]

It all starts with oneself. Getting detached from being attached to one's own ideas is tough, I must admit! As with many

---

84   "Crystal Methods", Wikiversity, https://en.wikiversity.org/wiki/Crystal_Methods

85   TED, "How to turn a group of strangers into a team", YouTube, 14/June/18,   https://www.youtube.com/watch?v=3boKz0Exros

things, realising that is what's started to happen, awareness is the beginning.

Personal safety is like the instructions for an aeroplane air mask. "In case of an emergency, you must apply it first to yourself." Here are three pointers to assess right now your personal safety margins from both within and around you:

- Give and be given the tools and training to do the job to the best ability?

- Treat and be treated with respect and dignity?

- Give recognition to and receive it from those you respect?

"If we could change ourselves, the tendencies in the world would also change. As a man changes his own nature, so does the attitude of the world change towards him. ... We need not wait to see what others do." - Mahatma Gandhi[86]

Be the change you want to see.

86   Mahatma. Gandhi, 1964, "General Knowledge About Health XXXII: Accidents Snake-Bite", *The Collected Works of Mahatma Gandhi, Volume XII, April 1913 to December 1914*, The Publications Division, Ministry of Information and Broadcasting, Government of India, http://www.gandhiheritageportal.org/the-collected-works-of-mahatma-gandhi

Tip

With this chapter story in mind, an aside to having the bare minimum of decency, manners and empathy to your colleagues... Rather than finger-pointing at individuals, it's clear that something has been lost there causing system failure. It's the system that has failed in the story you just heard.

I doubt very much that those individuals in and out of the team that were losing their temper would consider themselves bad people, but what they hadn't recognised was they had caved into pressure and lost their path.

The thing is, certain assumptions about motivation are ingrained in our society, for example the reward system built around 'carrots and sticks'[87]; *if you do X you get Y.* This way of 'motivating' encourages very short-term thinking at the cost of course, of the not-too-distant future.

If you are a leader, your job is to give your team the tools and support they need to get the job done and to work hard to minimise the things that get in their way.

---

87   "Carrot and Stick", Wikipedia, https://en.wikipedia.org/wiki/Carrot_and_stick

"I never teach my pupils; I only attempt to provide the conditions in which they can learn." - Albert Einstein[88]

It's time to break apart from this archaic model of rewards and punishment and work towards enabling an environment which encourages and praises autonomy, mastery and purpose[89].

"Picking values to live by it's the easy part; putting them into practice requires extraordinary attentiveness and persistence" - Marc Benioff, CEO of Salesforce[90]

Maybe, start with purpose. I've mentioned a few times *working together towards a common goal*, having clarity and direction on that goal and how that achieves a wider vision is key. Don't let it be fragmented, washed down or even forgotten.

At the beginning of your week's cycle with your grouplet, get the Product Owner to inject some energy and remind the direction of the product, and the fundamental reason for existence of the work. Then together craft the goal for that week and break down what is needed (feasible and reasonable) to accomplish it.

---

88   Albert Einstein, "Quotes by Albert Einstein", Good Reads, https://www.goodreads.com/quotes/253933-i-never-teach-my-pupils-i-only-attempt-to-provide

89   Daniel H. Pink, *Drive: The Surprising Truth About What Motivates Us*, (Edinburgh: Canongate Books Ltd., 2018)

90   Marc Benioff, *Trailblazer: The Power of Business as the Greatest Platform for Change*, (London: Simon & Schuster UK, 2019, https://www.salesforce.com/trailblazerbook/)

Why not try...

Over time even with best intentions on reducing quick 'tactical' solutions and workarounds, there is a certain amount of team effort invested in business-as-usual activities.

The experiment here starts with: watching the workload, making it visual and quantifying it.

How much of it is repetitive work? Like things that we do which are not creative but recreated. I call these 'boring things'.

As a team *shuffles* the boring things up, they are most likely less thrilling than others to tackle so let's avoid the same team member always ending up with it.

It's not just to share the pain but by rotation of repetitive work can unfold what it's really about: something which is clearly systematic. And what do we do with systematic things? We automate them! Hell yeah!

And if you're thinking 'we'll never get the time for it', well, quantifying the recurring 'boring things' gives you some figures to base it on. Elevate those boring things so that the cognitive effort can be applied to bringing value instead.

Put everyone into a room for a hands-on session, like a hackathon[91] for example. By the end of the session you can answer, with a working prototype, how you and your team elevate and alleviate those efforts. And automate the heck out of them!

"Passion is one great force that unleashes creativity, because if you're passionate about something, then you're more willing to take risks." - Yo-Yo Ma[92]

91   "Hackathon", Wikipedia, https://en.wikipedia.org/wiki/Hackathon

92   Yo Yo Ma, quoted by Philip Ball, "In Pursuit of NeuroScience: Yo Yo Ma", FT Magazine, 16/November/11, https://www.ft.com/content/af5633c4-de78-11e0-a2c0-00144feabdc0

Semantics

We must stay away from those 'carrots and sticks' as mentioned earlier as a reward-and-punishment system and also stay away from the terrible habit of controlling by authority imposition.

Instead of using phrases like 'we have to', phrase items around the purpose such as 'the aim here is to', 'we define our goal as', 'the objective is, 'what we are trying to achieve is' or 'we want to' etc.

Putting the emphasis on the end goal, rather than the 'how to'. Therefore supporting the wider purpose over oneself, accentuating autonomy around the 'how to get there'. By doing so, please promote **getting better at what we do**, perhaps by the use of some tools and functionality the team is interested in trying out, with the focus on skilling up towards mastery.

Are you willing to give it a try?

Book

Drive: The surprising truth of what motive us - Daniel H. Pink[93]

This book reinforces that motivation is intrinsic, that it comes from within and that we often subconsciously use the 'carrots and sticks' or 'if, then' reward system. There is much to be unlearned and much to embrace to become safer and happier whilst and beyond delivering Salesforce.

---

93   Daniel H. Pink, *Drive: The Surprising Truth About What Motivates Us*, (Edinburgh: Canongate Books Ltd., 2018)

Face-to-Face goes a Long Way

"The most efficient and effective method of conveying information to and within a development team is face-to-face conversation."
- Agile Manifesto[94]

---

94   Jim Highsmith, "History: The Agile Manifesto", Agile Manifesto, 2001, https://agilemanifesto.org/history.html

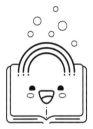

Begin to See the Light

Marco sat back on his chair and considered his options. As CEO of a hospitality company which was about to go through a restructure, it was his responsibility to manage the forthcoming changes in as considerate and forward-looking a way as possible.

The conclusion he came to was that releasing Salesforce concurrently with the restructure would both support the process of change and help with ongoing customer relationship management. It was important to Marco that staff be looked after and disruption kept to a minimum. He was confident that he'd made the right decision.

Six months later, however, things hadn't turned out as he'd hoped. The development and adoption of the Salesforce rollout had been massively hampered by the fact that the people looking after it had changed three times. Marco's vision for a smooth transition was looking imperilled.

To increase the usage of Salesforce, some Key Performance Indicators were put in place and cascaded to the users. Marco reasoned that this would encourage its use and support the staff. However, he hadn't factored that it wasn't only the software that had changed; many end users were still transitioning from previous roles, some were new to their job and some completely new to the industry.

One of the new Key Performance Indicators was a number of daily calls per user. The number was quite high in comparison to the amount being tracked in Salesforce at the time.

It really began as a figure to aspire to, yet within a couple of weeks it became the bare expected minimum 'or else'. People began to struggle.

"Why do I have the same KPI to meet in my small, winter venue as the team in the gigantic, year-round attraction? This is hospitality. Every venue is different. Different size, different volume, different seasonality." Abby, a Regional Manager was explaining to Marco some of the problems they were having. "Making daily calls has become the focal point of my team's workload, which is having a knock-on effect on other operations. People are worried they won't keep their jobs if they don't hit the magic number. It's compromising other work. Is that what you want?"

Malee joined in, "Do you realise, Marco, that because calls are also manually added into Salesforce as child records of either contacts or leads from purchased lists there is a greater margin of error; people are calling the same leads, leading to quantity over quality... bringing more layers of disruption."

Marco realised that something needed to change. He sent someone from the Salesforce team to work from each one of the sites instead of from head office. Head

> office was highly regarded but with certain decisions it seemed to be miles away from the day-to-day reality outside its walls. That move to be closer to the users within their daily environment and operations was a real eye-opener.

Talking and really listening to people makes a big difference, rather than waiting to put across 'our point'; we have two ears and one mouth for a reason so use it in its proportion.

When active listening happens face-to-face, it is even better as it brings another layer of richness in communication that wouldn't be happening otherwise.

Albert Mehrabian and his 7%-38%-55% Rule[95], attributes a 55% on body language for communication. Although the myths and flaws on the definition around that theory, other studies support that non-verbal communication certainly has a weighting to the totality of what and how we communicate. For example, a Harvard Business Review[96] supports that face-to-face is 34 times more successful than email.

The story talks to us about how easy it is to get alienated if there isn't an awareness to at the very least convey information, the most effective way to do that for humans is with a conversation. And I'd argue that it's also with visuals, we need to see it.

---

95   "Albert Mehrabian", Wikipedia, https://en.wikipedia.org/wiki/Albert_Mehrabian

96   Vanessa K. Bohns, "A Face-to-Face Request Is 34 Times More Successful Than an Email", Harvard Business Review, 11/April/17, https://hbr.org/2017/04/a-face-to-face-request-is-34-times-more-successful-than-an-email

"Everything for me is visual. That's just how my head works" - Whoopi Goldberg[97]

After all, this is how our brain processes information, how we form memories and how we recall them[98]. With visuals, seeing things, it's not just easier to digest but also it's proven that we can't read and listen at the same time[99].

Being closer, present, with conversation and seeing; surfaces an understanding of the day-to-day that wouldn't have been grasped any other way.

"Leaving things at the intuition level makes communication almost impossible" - Eliyahu M. Goldratt[100]

How many times have you been in a meeting where at the end someone asks, "are we all in agreement?", "do we all understand?" and then everyone answers "yes" but actually everyone has a different understanding of what the agreement is?

97   Whoopi Goldberg, as interviewed by Mekado Murphy, "Tribeca Film Festival Q. and A.: Whoopi Goldberg", The New York Times, 23/April/13, https://artsbeat.blogs.nytimes.com/2013/04/23/tribeca-film-festival-qa-whoopi-goldberg/

98   Erin McCoy, "How Our Brains Are Hardwired for Visual Content", Killer Visual Strategies, 21/February/19, https://killervisualstrategies.com/blog/how-our-brains-are-hardwired-for-visual-content.html

99   Linda Carroll, "Your brain can't swipe, browse and hear at the same time, scans show", Health, 8/December/15, https://www.today.com/health/your-brain-cant-swipe-hear-same-time-scans-show-t60356

100   Eliyahu M. Goldratt, "Preview — Theory of Constraints", Good Reads, https://www.goodreads.com/en/book/show/582174.Theory_of_Constraints

Visuals are super powerful assets to convey common understanding, rather than leaving agreements at the intuition level, helps to express it in a way that is easier to understand, digest and recall. Visuals are not only good for explaining things to others but I find them quite useful for myself to organise my thoughts as I present the content.

I use visuals in meetings all the time. I even spin them on the spot so we can *draw* the concept by hand together in a collaborative way where everyone can see the same thing. Also, all these visuals become tangible artifacts from the meeting that we can then share and refer back to.

Now I'll be deviating into working from anywhere, and doing so very consciously as this is a subject that I feel very passionate about. And yes, working from anywhere doesn't stop us being face-to-face.

I continue to write this during the 2020 COVID19[101] first peak in Europe as so many events and conferences have moved to virtual settings and I assume that **most** jobs right now are happening in remote environments. Many organisations have been forced into it and, with them, individuals too. I dare to predict that beyond this pandemic working from home or

---

101   "COVID-19 Pandemic", Wikipedia, https://en.wikipedia.org/wiki/COVID-19_pandemic

working from anywhere will be the 'new normal', a *better* normal.

Although the circumstances are often difficult, the fact of working in a remote setting does not remove the ability to have those face-to-face interactions. We have the means and technology to do so!

Tip

I have been working for years with distributed teams and that comes in many shapes or forms. To my surprise, within the second week of March 2020, there was already a boom in 'tips and tricks' about working from home. I really thought it was a much more common practice by now, especially with the work that we do. Cloud anyone?

Distributed does not mean dispersed.

Now, I do understand that it may come with the need for some adjustment, as it also would be when moving offices or changing teams. The interactions need to be redefined for the new environment.

All changes come with opportunities and working remotely brings a range of possibilities and extra time, and time is a perishable good. On the individual's level, think of all that time gained by not commuting! But also think, on the team's level, how a remote setting can serve as an opportunity to support focus and the concept of flow we discussed earlier.

The tip here would be to have an agreement for working arrangements, and encourage face-to-face interactions. That translates to the tech that we have on hand: turn your camera on!

And yes, nowadays you can blur the background or have any image there; but for myself, honestly, I just leave it as it is. By having 'the real background' it brings another layer, for example my clients finding out about my love for board games. Get to see your teams, regardless of whether your colleague's children are playing in the background. Who cares? This is us.

Look at each other's faces, and appreciate the expressions and all that comes with that. It does make a difference.

Why not try...

The experiment for this chapter goes in line with the working agreements and working remotely yet supporting face-to-face interactions.

It's one of the things that I've tried a couple of times and has seemed to work nicely for the team. Inspired by an idea seen and experienced within the Salesforce MVP community: at times, out of the blue, a fellow MVP posts a link in a channel we have in common and opens it up for anybody to join, just like that. So the experiment expansion of that is:

Have an all-day team link.

Enable a virtual room during working hours, all-day every-day, that people can join at any point. It's multipurpose really, it serves to: ask questions, have a virtual coffee, a team lunch, bounce ideas off each other, etc.

You may observe that it will come and go in waves, starting as a novelty with much attention, gradually becoming quieter and picking up throughout different delivery times... and that's okay. It's there as and when needed, a space **for** the team, led **by** the team.

Semantics

The word remote itself has connotations of being distant and being far. Although we may not be in close physical proximity, we can still be near, present and on-hand for our teamies, working together towards the common goal.

As I mentioned earlier my prediction is that working as a distributed team will be the new normal. Why? It's better for the environment, it offers everyone flexibility, you get time back to invest in yourself instead of your commute, it's an attractor for professionals and gives organisations the ability to look at a global talent pool.

Therefore I'd suggest referring to the setting as '*distributed*' rather than '*remote*'. Distributed teams can take many shapes and forms, some colocated, some *satellite*… call it anything but '*remote*'. Why does it even need a name? There is no need to even say we work *remotely*...

We work, punto!

Book

From Chaos to Successful Distributed Agile Teams: Collaborate to Deliver - Johanna Rothman and Mark Kilby[102]

An honest and straight-to-the-point read talking about the concept of distribution in the work space. It covers the principles of supporting teams and at scale so that it can be successful. Among many highlights, my top highlight was that Johanna and Mark both applied the concepts in the book to themselves whilst writing it. Now, that's leading by example! Experiment with yourself and practise what you preach.

---

102   Johanna Rothman and Mark Kilby, *From Chaos To Successful Distributed Agile Teams*, (Practical Ink, 2015)

Measure Progress by Working Product

"Working software is the primary measure of progress."
- Agile Manifesto[103]

---

103   Jim Highsmith, "History: The Agile Manifesto", Agile Manifesto, 2001, https://agilemanifesto.org/history.html

Barking Up the Wrong Tree

The Salesforce ecosystem has grown at an incredible pace. Because of this, the demand for support for Salesforce customers has also grown, which has provided a plethora of opportunities for creating companies to support that demand.

One such consultancy had been set up by a brother and sister team, and this family feel was part of what made it successful. Christie and her brother Ben understood each other and worked together well. Their customers appreciated feeling part of a tight-knit group and things were going well.

Even as they expanded, slowly at first, and brought on their first few new team members the family feel wasn't lost. Christie and Ben worked closely with everyone and made sure their vision was understood.

New colleagues always got the same talk from Christie. "Bill hours. Bill hours. Bill hours. The more hours you bill, the more revenue we get. The more revenue we get, the more potential we have for growth. The more we grow, the more people we can bring on board. The more people we can bring on board, the more competitive we are. The more competitive we are, the more successful we are. The process of success is built on a foundation of billing hours."

Ben would then explain, "Every week we have a team review where we look at the hours we've all worked. I cannot stress to you enough that this is our focus."

At that stage, the company only had a couple of customers. Christie and Ben were able to fully focus on those customers and help them to extend their Salesforce orgs. They knew their customers' businesses intimately, after all, they held so much institutional knowledge in their heads, and were easily accessible; two things which were very much appreciated and becoming a unique selling point in a world of big organisations.

It didn't take long for clashes to emerge between the 'bill hours, bill hours, bill hours' mantra of an expanding team and the family-run business ethos. Customers started to raise concerns about the increase in the hours they were being billed for and the lack of delivered solutions when compared with the service they were used to receiving.

Christie and Ben were having a bit of a crisis meeting. "What do we do, Ben? Our team isn't just new to us, most of them are new to Salesforce technology as well. They mean well, but their lack of experience and reliance on each other is slowing things down."

"We need to stick to our plan, Chris. Billing hours is key. Let's get the team to also add detailed descriptions of what they do to their hourly logs. We can share those with customers, if necessary. That should help build confidence?"

Ben's suggestion was cascaded to the team. The importance of billing hours was reiterated and it was explained that they would now have to keep detailed records of how they had spent their time.

There was nervousness in the air. Team members stopped asking each other for help. They were reluctant to jump into calls together. They stopped seeking or offering support in any way which could be perceived as demonstrating lack of knowledge or skill, in case it aggravated customers even more.

The 'bill more...success' upward spiral irrevocably changed direction and became a spiral of self-destruction. Let's leave it at that.

Pluralsight[104] LIVE Europe 2020[105] had an excellent keynote from Sue Perkins on her tech and comedy insights, which couldn't have come at a better time for me as I watched it hours from writing this. I leave you here with a quotation which comes in quite handy for this story:

"If a business isn't founded on love and respect and decency, it isn't a business worth belonging to. We have to find our tribe, the people, the employers who reflect our values." - Sue Perkins

With 'businesses' meaning to me each and every component—team, department, site, project, product—and these being the foundations out of which the overall operating system is made.

Although I often hear that teams don't have a choice, let me tell you something: you do have a choice and a say in everything you do! And like with any other thing, validate your thoughts with an empirical process, verifying by experience rather than pure theory. Try it, measure and decide what's the next step.

---

104   Pluralsight is an online education company that offers video training courses for software developers, IT administrators, and creative professionals through its website.

105   "The Ultimate Tech Skills Conference", PLURAL-SIGHT, https://www.pluralsight.com/live-europe

Ultimately, what matters is getting that value into the market, into the hands of the users. The metrics should reflect that, or else it drives unwanted results. Such as in both this and the previous story, we do need to be careful with what and how we measure.

"Hours themselves represent a cost. Instead, measure output. Who cares how many hours someone worked on something? All that matters is how fast it's delivered and how good it is." - Jeff Sutherland[106]

You can observe in most organisations today the biggest waste is time, to my observations time wasted on mainly two activities:

- Progress Updates: Where are we right now? What's the difference between where we are and the initial plan? Things change. Plans become obsolete as things unfold. I'd challenge the relevance of the progress updates vs initial plan.

- Prioritisation: As previously mentioned the importance of prioritisation, I see so often the huge demand of time, effort and intelligence across an organisation in an attempt to predict the future, 12 or even 18 months in advance, before any work even starts.

It's draining, and often charged by personal agendas and polarisation of ideas to find a 'happy' medium, a compromise. What it actually does is divert all that time, effort and intelligence away from delivering anything! Diverting away from delivering what's really needed to sustain the future of the business.

Lean prioritisation should be based on experiments. Just like science, create a hypothesis from the vision, break each one into predictions and validate them with the smallest possible

106   Jeff Sutherland, *Scrum: The Art of Doing Twice the Work in Half the Time*, (London: Random House Business Books, 2015)

effort. This tells you whether you should persevere or try something else.

This may all sound like 'big dreams' but validation and monitoring is very specific and should be embedded in everything we do.

For example, think about the build in Salesforce for the communities product: case deflection component[107], where community users get served with previously solved questions of other users or your own content of knowledge articles as they are typing the subject of a new case. That's the functionality but doesn't stop there, as if you also install the reports package on communities you can then monitor how the feature of case deflection performs, therefore helping you to move away to draw conclusions based on correlation and gut feeling so that you can validate the effectiveness of the feature release.

Similarly look at how the in-built Salesforce Lightning Usage app[108], where you can see how Lightning is performing and how the users are behaving with the application, also if and when they switch to prior experience.

Let's learn from this, and build monitoring and validation in each thing, every new product, feature, marketing campaign, sales offer or new proposition…

Prioritisation needs to be based on, and validated against, real observations and measurements. In other words, it needs to be data-driven and evidence-based. Another common word for this in scientific circles is 'empirical'[109].

---

107   "Case Deflection", Salesforce, https://help.salesforce.com/articleView?id=rss_case_deflection.htm&type=5

108   "Get Lightning Experience Adoption Insights with the Lightning Usage App", Salesforce, https://help.salesforce.com/articleView?id=lex_lightning_usage_app.htm&type=5

109   Empirical (adjective): "Based on, concerned with, or verifiable by observation or experience rather than theory or pure logic.", Lexico, https://www.lexico.com/definition/empirical

Keep constant **focus**. As one of the Scrum values, this reminds us to keep our eyes on the goal. With monitoring and validation we can reduce deviation from the goal. We learn from Crystal[110] that focus is also referring to the direction and to maximise the flow and avoid disruption.

110   "Crystal Methods", Wikiversity, https://en.wikiversity. org/wiki/Crystal_Methods

Tip

One thing that's very powerful is making work visible by using a board to represent work in progress. Just there, on the board, is the reinforcement of the team's common goal. Use it to guide the team to focus towards the goal, to tune and adjust to achieve it.

Other metrics you may want to make visible and fine tune with your team over time are highlighted in the State of DevOps Report[111], such as:

- Lead Time: how long does it take from inception to delivery? And how can the team refine it to be shorter? That may need influence on external factors to the team in question.

- Deployment Frequency: how often do you deploy to production? And how can the team refine it to be shorter? Here, items such as automation tests, packaging and deployment pipeline make the difference.

111   Nicole Forsgren et al., "State of DevOps 2019", Google Services, https://services.google.com/fh/files/misc/state-of-devops-2019.pdf

- Time to Restore: how long does it take to restore the service after a failure? And how can the team refine it to be shorter? Supporting to create a safer environment for all.

- Change Fail: the rate at which changes to production have degraded the service and consequently hotfixes or rollbacks applied, how can the team refine it to be smaller? Therefore supporting safety.

- Availability: uptime of the system in question and how can the team constantly work towards 99.999% (so-called "five nines"[112]), it's a journey not a destination.

These are derived from the industry-standard the Four Key Metrics[113], adding availability as an important component to recognise the outcome and co-create value.

To add to that, the common idea of earlier issue discovery the less expensive it is, shifting left. Therefore, discovering defects early[114] in your development pipeline is less expensive than having to fix them further down the line, production bugs being the most expensive not only "in money terms" but in stress levels and trust.

If you are going to measure something, measure what fosters a working environment that tangibly helps to bring that value sooner in a safer and happier way.

---

112   The gold standard is the so-called "five nines" availability (99.999%) - "Percentage Calculation", Wikipedia, https://en.wikipedia.org/wiki/High_availability#Percentage_calculation

113   "Four key metrics - Technology Radar", Thought Works, https://www.thoughtworks.com/radar/techniques/four-key-metrics

114   "Discover Defects Early", Wiki, 15/May/18, https://wiki.c2.com/?DiscoverDefectsEarly

Why not try...

Research[115] shows that multitasking has a detrimental effect on efficiency, especially on complicated matters, as it takes additional time to shift focus.

The experiment here is to do one project at the time.

Yes I did say that, avoid the waste that context switching brings, and supercharge with focus and flow.

Otherwise what essentially happens is the expansion of the effort, yet no value delivered. Plus the longer time elapses the more expensive it is to refine, both in time and money. A partially done something increases financial risk and waste.

Re-work is also rather detrimental not just to a project but to oneself. For more on this you may want to explore the concepts of Lean Manufacturing[116] and its focus on reduction of

115   Isabel Gauthier, "Journal of Experimental Psychology: Human Perception and Performance", APA, https://www.apa.org/pubs/journals/xhp/index

116   "Lean Manufacturing", Wikipedia, https://en.wikipedia.org/wiki/Lean_manufacturing

waste. I'd recommend the book, *The Machine That Changed the World*[117].

With this theme, as with others, start with yourself. Look at your workspace setup, reduce notifications, block sections to achieve specific goals, reduce distractions and allow yourself to get into deep flow (see page 60).

---

117   James P. Womack, Daniel T. Jones and Daniel Roos, The Machine That Changed the World, (London: Simon & Schuster UK, Ltd., 2007)

Semantics

Track *outcomes* over outputs, that being *results* over indicators. Do the shift of focus to the effects of the efforts, that's where the value is found.

Here I'd point you to further research and inspiration on the concept of Objectives and Key Results (OKRs)[118] and move away from Key Performance Indicators (KPIs) and create your own thing to align focus on effort towards common goals.

---

118   "OKRs",   Wikipedia,   https://en.wikipedia.org/wiki/OKR

Book

Scrum: The Art of Doing Twice the Work in Half the Time - Jeff Sutherland[119]

With a rather controversial title, this book takes you through the inception of Scrum framework to what it is today, getting things done for better and sooner value. The book is filled with real life stories that force the concepts and how it is used in rather innovative ways and unthought industries.

---

119   Jeff Sutherland, *Scrum: The Art of Doing Twice the Work in Half the Time*, (London: Random House Business Books, 2015)

Sustainable Pace

"Agile processes promote sustainable development. The sponsors, developers, and users should be able to maintain a constant pace indefinitely." - Agile Manifesto[120]

---

120   Jim Highsmith, "History: The Agile Manifesto", Agile Manifesto, 2001, https://agilemanifesto.org/history.html

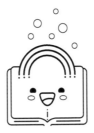

There's No Such Thing
as a Free Lunch

They were known as The Four Musketeers. Binta, Andrew, Jo and Moki were a Salesforce Developer, two Salesforce Administrators and a Data Analyst who looked after more than a thousand users and five separate Salesforce instances. These Salesforce instances included one which was huge, with global operations and hundreds of users mainly focused on servicing, and a range of others which varied from local goods to a travel agency. Working across these multiple instances was their bread-and-butter work, day in and day out. Their 'business as usual' activities took up more than 75% of their capacity in a good week.

One Thursday, Binta came back from a meeting and explained to the rest of the team that they needed to get ready for some extra work. "As you know, there have recently been extensive changes at the leadership level. The new honchos have brought new ideas, and they're looking for digital solutions to help to implement them.

Our reputation and skills mean we're going to be in demand, particularly as Salesforce is the most widely used application across all businesses."

"OK, B, this sounds like a job for the Four Musketeers, for sure!" Andrew, Jo and Moki were up for the task; they were proud to be so highly regarded and confident in their abilities.

They hadn't, however, accounted for what the extra work would look like in practice.

Moki sighed as Andrew and Jo came back from yet another meeting. "What extra work have you brought back this time? You want me to solve the climate crisis? Produce world peace?" It was becoming a running joke that not only were they spending more time than ever at meetings, but each meeting would produce a pile of new work.

"You can moan, Moki, but it won't change the fact that we're going to have to keep coming in earlier and leaving later just to stay vaguely on top of things. We've got to attend the ideation discussions for new functionality and somehow implement everyone's new ideas. Doesn't anyone realise we've still got all the work we originally had?" Jo's frustrations were really starting to bubble to the surface.

For a good couple of months the team worked like Trojans.

Andrew let out an exhausted groan. "People are starting to demand that we deliver on their new ideas. They don't understand how much else we've got on and how hard we're working. We know that none of these ideas are on their way to production. We're doing our best!" He aired his disquiet to the team, but knew that he was just voicing what they were all feeling.

Once again, it fell to Binta to pass on the suggestions from the leadership team. "They want us to drop some of our other activities, including internal reporting. We're going to support this particular drop by running training sessions across the globe, so that users can self-serve. I know that this is going to push us in to weekend working, but it can't be helped."

Although Andrew and Jo weren't keen to work weekends, they could see that showing users how to report themselves would be a useful way to free up some of their time. However, like the best laid plans, it didn't quite work out like that.

Rather than spread the workload, delegating reports to users meant that things were suddenly being done in myriad different ways. Individuals filtered reports in their own quirky styles, which led to an influx of requests related to report discrepancies.

Working life continued like this. More and more demands and no consideration of how those demands would be met, or indeed whether they could be. It should have come as no surprise to anyone when, in close succession, Binta, Andrew and Moki all gave notice. They simply couldn't carry on working in that way and the employment market was so good that they all pretty much walked into new jobs with better terms.

Their organisation made counter offers to all of them, and to hire more people, but it was too late. They had completely burnt out.

Please note from the story's ending that increasing the team size does not necessarily translate into a higher speed of delivery[121]. I observe this anti-pattern frequently. The obvious reason is that the team will, no matter what, slow down first for

---

121   "The Mythical Man-Month", Wikipedia, https://en.wikipedia.org/wiki/The_Mythical_Man-Month

adjusting to the change and for things like knowledge transfer, setup, ramping up and more.

But also more people means that the communication options increase and the human brain can't handle it beyond a certain point. It generates too much repetition which can lead to miscommunication, flow disruption and context switch, all of which is waste.

Remember the grouplets? The Scrum framework recommends[122] a team size of seven (plus or minus two). See below how the lines of communication exponentially increase when increasing team size:

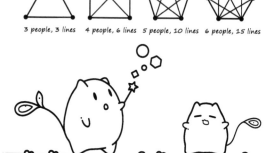

3 people, 3 lines   4 people, 6 lines   5 people, 10 lines   6 people, 15 lines

On the subject of overload of communication, nowadays there are just so many ways to reach your colleagues. This can generate anxiety and lack of focus so we must be mindful of others and ourselves. Make sure you all agree on the subject, for example: which tool for which purpose and when?

Whilst reading the story you may have thought that 75%, for a team effort going into business-as-usual activities, is way too much. In principle, I'd agree. But you will be surprised to

---

122   Filip Lewandowski, "Development Team Size", Scrum, https://www.scrum.org/forum/scrum-forum/5759/development-team-size

know how much effort, time and intelligence goes into repetitive tasks for anyone, for any team and for any organisation.

One thing you can do is gather data. Gathering data around it and representing it visually, helps realisation and it should prompt conversations on how to elevate the repetitive efforts that are high volume into more systematic, automated and/or self-served solutions (as we spoke about in our story). A system that needs so much manual intervention is just not sustainable over time.

Also, as we touched on earlier in the book, teams can go fast, real fast! But if the rest of the organisation doesn't keep up, it defeats the object. Because an organisation is an operating system in itself, to perform at its best it requires attention to the interactions, system thinking.

"What's happening isn't an averaging out of the fluctuations in our various speeds, but an accumulation of the fluctuations. And mostly it's an accumulation of slowness - because dependency limits the opportunities for higher fluctuations. And that's why the line is spreading" - Eliyahu M. Goldratt[123]

To break through that we need courage. One more value of Extreme programming. **Courage**[124] *"Is the commandment to always design and code for today and not for tomorrow. This is an effort to avoid getting bogged down in design and requiring a lot of effort to implement anything else."* This also means persistence, refactoring and speaking up. Courage, as a Scrum value, is about doing the right thing and working on tough problems.

"Life shrinks or expands in proportion to one's courage" - Anaïs Nin[125]

---

123   Eliyahu M. Goldratt, *What is this Thing Called Theory of Constraints*, (North River Press), https://www.amazon.com/What-Thing-Called-Theory-Constraints/dp/B0029IEYHQ

124   "Extreme Programming", Wikipedia, https://en.wikipedia.org/wiki/Extreme_programming#Values

125   Anaïs Nin, quoted in Carol A. Dingle, *Memorable Quotations: French Writers of the Past*, (Lincoln: iUniverse, 2000)

Tip

And being sustainable is not just about the product itself that we deliver to endure over time but also it's about the people involved, just like in the story. Being overworked or underworked is just nonsense. It's not good for your health, focus, concentration, happiness, effectiveness… and it can't be maintained over time. In other words, it's unsustainable.

Working long hours, long weeks and long months doesn't get more done. And certainly whatever is done is not necessarily better. On the contrary, if you ask me, it tends to be much lower in quality.

It's a draining pace that has a detrimental effect on mood, stamina, intelligence and your whole life. Remember that life is perishable, we should treat every moment with the care that it deserves. Being ephemeral, it ain't coming back. So look after yourself, go home and switch off; help your team and the rest of your organisation to do the same.

Psychological safety is becoming more and more important because it's all intertwined. A supporting area is making failure acceptable. That includes you as an enabler, to make smarter investments in things like tooling and reducing technical debt.

"There is only one thing that makes a dream impossible to achieve: the fear of failure" - Paulo Coelho[126]

Fear of failure is a very common silent enemy and requires 'unlearning' years of experience so that each and every one of us can and wants to speak up, open up to each other including weaknesses and flaws, and learn from each other or else forget about innovation.

What are the consequences of pushing too hard beyond one's self and the team's limits?

---

126   Paulo Coelho, *The Alchemist*, (New York: Harper San Francisco, 1988)

Why not try...

I'm sorry to break this to you but... we can't foresee the future and we are very bad at predicting and estimating it. Even with uncertainty we are better at assessing and comparing smaller and closer in-time events.

So let's try something out. At the beginning of your week's cycle, come together with your grouplet and with the product vision in mind to craft a goal for that week, and discuss what can realistically be done. Even discuss how it can be done, breaking down some of the work and most importantly opening up conversations. Remember, there is always more than one way to achieve something and the value lies in the interactions.

Perhaps someone is aware of some intricacies of the application or related to it for the team to be mindful of, or maybe there is the option to reuse some frameworks already in place that may make it easier and better in the long run.

Coming together with your grouplet at the start of your cycle is known as Sprint Planning[127].

---

127   "What is Sprint Planning", Scrum, https://www.scrum.org/resources/what-is-sprint-planning

When you look at the roughly defined and agreed work, ask is it ready? Does the team have all they need to start? And very importantly, how will we know when each piece towards the goal is done? Remember that work expands so try to avoid items becoming a never ending story.

Not only that but the concept of *planning* gives those fresh starts (Ref page 73) the boost of starting together. We are after all, social beings. The diversity within the team and also what we have in common. Make the most of starting together and starting often.

Semantics

After all, the goal is not to be 'Agile', the goal is to improve. I came across the following description from Jon Smart which really resonates with me, the goal is to get: Better Value Sooner Safer Happier[128] and it's a journey not a destination.

Use those five words in your day to day. Better over best, value over output, sooner over faster, safer over hurried, and happier the one that we seem to forget yet makes all the difference.

128   IT Revolution, "Better Value Sooner Safer Happier - Jon Smart", YouTube, 1/July/19, https://www.youtube.com/watch?v=ZKrhdyjGoM8

Book

The Hen That Laid the Golden Eggs[129]
- Aesop's Fables

I could not resist referring to this fable all the time as it simply explains how greed and narrow-mindedness defeat the effort. As does having an unsustainable pace, your product will not hold over time nor your team. Ultimately the aim is to deliver Better Value Sooner Safer Happier, if any are questionable then challenge it as it most likely won't be worth the effort.

---

129   Aesop, *The Complete Fables*, trans. Robert Temple and Olivia Temple, (London: Penguin, 1988)

Pursuit Design and Technical Excellence

"Continuous attention to technical excellence and good design enhances agility." - Agile Manifesto[130]

---

130   Jim Highsmith, "History: The Agile Manifesto", Agile Manifesto, 2001, https://agilemanifesto.org/history.html

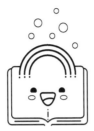

A Stitch in Time Saves Nine

Four years after Lightning[131] was first announced, an eight year old Salesforce instance was due to make its transition.

In general many customers have resisted this change. The truth is that it wasn't just the user interface which needed an uplift, but the modularity and elasticity that Lightning brings were an important part too. It's a difficult one to gain agreement and headspace on; there is a cost attached but some people found it hard to see how it could bring or retain customers or how it could reduce or protect costs. Arguably, however, it could do all these things.

Making this transition was the undercover mission of Frankie and her team. The instance they were transitioning had around 800 users, and it was Frankie's team's job to make this transition happen with no impact on any other work.

Frankie was uber-experienced at working with Salesforce and started this mission by running the multiple

---

131   "Salesforce Lightning: The Future of Sales and CRM", Salesforce, https://www.salesforce.com/uk/campaign/lightning/

tools[132] provided, such as the readiness check, visualforce scan and optimizer as well as many others. She understood that such a huge job needed to be prioritised and segmented, so broke down the items that needed attention into tiny stories which she and the team then worked on. Remembering the parable of the jar full of rocks which could still be filled with pebbles and then sand, they worked on the principle that breaking things down meant that everything could get done, bit by bit, sprint by sprint, without having an impact on other deliverables.

Some of their sprints didn't make much progress. Other things were fluctuating and she didn't want them to be compromised. In general, however, by completing one tiny story after another they were making headway.

Around her, the team could feel the rhythm of progress. There was minimal risk from their tweaks as no users yet had been given access to the Lightning interface in production. They could deliver these small changes which didn't affect users with each release without worry about knock-on consequences.

Some tweaks—those which would have had an impact on users—weren't delivered with the standard releases and instead landed in a separate sandbox environment. Although a separate sandbox is not necessarily a problem, the team found themselves in a situation where they were diverting release after release from production long after they had completed the main development. Uh-oh.

Uh-oh, indeed. Let's fast forward our story to a sprint planning meeting with only two sprints left to go live. Paulo, one of the Salesforce Developers, raised con-

---

132   "Lightning Experience Transition Tools", App Exchange,   https://appexchange.salesforce.com/mktcollections/cloud-collections/Lightning

cerns that deployment would be really hard going and that many people would be taken by surprise. It finally dawned on everyone that, although they'd felt that there was momentum and progress, the changes in the separate sandbox hadn't been tracked and weren't in line with other deployments or in any code repository.

Should they try to merge all the code and work through the errors? Or revisit the stories one at a time and replicate? Or some other solution yet to be considered? They were in real trouble.

Salesforce is great for many reasons, one is the concept of citizen development[133]. The ability to enhance the application with low code, clicks, drag and drop configuration. Now, it has its advantages with tons of ready to use functionality, you don't have to write unit tests (although I argue that we should) and it's low maintenance as Salesforce does the heavy lifting for you. But with great power comes great responsibility.

You have to track your changes! You must isolate what you are deploying, which is each particular change. Even if that change is manual, track it. As some of the things for example in the setup menu, you may not know exactly which type of metadata you are changing. The trickier it gets as the faster you go and the more changes you perform. Version control is the one thing that can make it or break it.

The concept of DevOps[134] is here to save you trouble, and it's unquestionably part of your pursuit of technical excellence.

---

133   John Everhard, "The Pros and Cons of Citizen Development", *Forbes*, 22/January/19, https://www.forbes.com/sites/johneverhard/2019/01/22/the-pros-and-cons-of-citizen-development/#56e912c484fd

134   DevOps term can be defined as developers looking after their apps in production by taking on more sysadmin duties; and operators developing tools to automate their tasks, reduce manual work and increase reassurance.

Via Trailhead[135] you have an introduction into Application Lifecycle and Development Models[136]. Pay extra attention to the last module: 'Use Package Development for More Flexible Releases'.

Even when you operate in the tiny stories size nirvana, they get bundled in releases and more often than not in big releases. So how can you decouple to enable continuous delivery? How do you help your future self with loosely coupled architecture? For example look at how it can help to reduce dependencies, agnostics of other areas, enabling changing the underlying tech without affecting the application, easier to automate tests as the modules have a single purpose, independently deployable can also fail independently...

The earlier mentioned State of DevOps report (See page 131) is an insightful year-to-year reading of how across the industry the concept and its practices evolve and the challenges it faces. From the latest report it seems obvious that speed, stability and availability enable better performance as an organisation, which includes profit; productivity and customer satisfaction.

The team in our story learnt, albeit pretty painfully, that speed — regardless of how big or small — without control is reckless. The changes in the separate sandbox should have been tracked and even with a simple branching model it could have been validated against future deployments, the automation suite updated and run as part of the process.

The other thing worth noting around technical excellence is the concept of multi-tenancy[137] in Salesforce, so you will have to manage things such as governor limits, processing time,

---

135   "What Is Trailhead?", Salesforce, https://help.salesforce. com/articleView?id=mth_what_is_trailhead.htm&type=5

136   "Application Lifecycle and Development Models", Trailhead,   https://trailhead.salesforce.com/en/content/learn/ modules/application-lifecycle-and-development-models

137   "Multi Tenant Architecture", Salesforce, https://devel- oper.salesforce.com/page/Multi_Tenant_Architecture

number of queries and data manipulation statements, which are limits in the utilisation of the platform. Although it may feel like a bit of a 'logistics manoeuvre', the constraints are in place to look after the common infrastructure, and that is part of having a robust and secure Salesforce instance. It is part of the job to have attention to technical excellence, good design and constant refinement. One could argue that architecture emerges[138].

Another common property we learn from Crystal[139], **Technical environment** with automated tests, configuration management, and frequent integration. Highlighting the importance of version control, checking-in code into a repository to identify problems to revert or correct it and how configuration management and automation tests helps there.

Just recently Salesforce announced a DevOps Center[140] functionality to help Salesforce development teams (working with both clicks and code) to collaborate to deliver sooner and safer. Think of the DevOps Center like an app, a release management app. This environment is to be connected to your Source Code Repository, so once you are done you can 'Pull Changes' with the click of a button.

---

138   Mile Hyson, "Can An Architecture Emerge", Wiki, 24/September/12, https://wiki.c2.com/?CanAnArchitectureEmerge

139   "Crystal Methods", Wikiversity, https://en.wikiversity.org/wiki/Crystal_Methods

140   "Salesforce Introduces New Developer Tools for Building, Scaling, and Shipping Apps", Salesforce, 23/June/20, https://www.salesforce.com/company/news-press/stories/2020/6/salesforce-developer-announcement/

Tip

You may have been in a scenario similar to our story team, where some items were ready to deploy but not ready yet for the users. In these situations what can one do? Having a long running separate branch and environment leads to diversion.

One of the things I have seen working well are Feature Flags also called a feature toggle[141]. So that you can have whatever it is you are working on when ready: deployed and hidden, with the flag you can enable or disable the feature so that it can be run with everything else and can also act as a safety net to switch off changes quickly if need be.

Remember to remove them once they have served their purpose. A cluttered instance with legacy logic is just asking for trouble.

"Good programmers write good code. Great programmers write no code. Zen programmers delete code" - John Byrd[142]

141   "Feature Toggle", Wikipedia, https://en.wikipedia.org/wiki/Feature_toggle

142   John Byrd, "What's Zen programming?", Quora, https://www.quora.com/John-Byrd-says-Good-programmers-write-good-code-Great-programmers-write-no-code-Zen-programmers-delete-code-Whats-Zen-programming

Why not try...

Technical excellence and good design is a journey, not a destination. Hence, it emerges. That reduction of technical debt[143] may not be the easiest to articulate to have a theme of work (or project) of its own, therefore it must be a part of the process.

And yes, you may be in a scenario where you push so-called tactical solutions out the door, but they are to be revisited afterwards to make them better and safer, or else they can easily fall into the forgotten land.

So, here's the experiment: Have a backlog.

"The Product Backlog is an ordered list of everything that is known to be needed in the product. It is the single source of requirements for any changes to be made to the product. The Product Owner is responsible for the Product Backlog, including its content, availability, and ordering. A Product Backlog is never complete."[144]

143   "Technical Debt", Wikipedia, https://en.wikipedia.org/wiki/Technical_debt

144   "What is a Product Backlog", Scrum, https://www.scrum.org/resources/what-is-a-product-backlog

As part of that backlog, include what helps you and your team to pursue technical excellence and good design. That should certainly be part of your product roadmap. Don't let it fall into the forgotten land.

Although the Product Owner is responsible for it, anyone can contribute to the backlog, so as a team just add things there that bring value. That includes hardening solutions already in place so that your product can be sustained over time.

Because of the backlogs' dynamic nature, they are ever-changing so try not to define it all. In a sense, the backlog is a one dimensional priority list so focus on defining the items at the very top and avoid waste doing anything beyond that as it will change, some items may not even be wanted or needed any more.

It's important to articulate to the Product Owner the benefits of that continuous attention to technical excellence and good design, ultimately it will support your product by generation or protection of revenue and by the reduction or protection of cost.

Semantics

How many times you have been in discussions where a big resistance comes from one of the parties, if you only get a 'no no no', more disagreement it will only generate a further polarisation of ideas. Even some resistant responses are disguised as 'yes, but', so be aware!

Try to build upon each other's ideas instead. Starting with oneself, exercise a 'Yes, and'[145], rather than responding with 'no' or 'yes, but'. Experiment with being an enabler rather than a blocker.

145   Iwona Winiarska, "Improv in Agile: Yes, And…", Winiarska, https://winiarska.com/blog/improv-in-agile-yes-and/

Book

Accelerate, The Science of Lean Software and DevOps - Nicole Forsgren, Jez Humble and Gene Kim[146]

This book explains how DevOps emerged to solve how to build secure, resilient, rapidly evolving distributed systems at scale. Which capabilities and paradigms are there to focus to continuously drive improvement.

All based on research from surveys of the State of DevOps report and outcomes of profitability, productivity & market share, it identifies 24 key capabilities that do make a difference. It clarifies concepts such as the difference of Continuous Integration and Continuous Delivery, how leadership can tangibly impact the so-called 'culture' with detailed and specific actions.

146   Nicole Forsgren, Jez Humble and Gene Kim, *Accelerate: The Science of Lean Software and DevOps*, (Portland: IT Revolution Press, 2018)

Keep Things Simple

"Simplicity – the art of maximizing the amount of work not done – is essential." - Agile Manifesto[147]

147   J. Highsmith, "History: The Agile Manifesto", Agile Manifesto, 2001, https://agilemanifesto.org/history.html

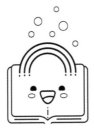

Waste Not, Want Not

Let me introduce you to a large training company which had, over the years, developed a purposeful matching system, based on skills, for all its areas: individuals, courses and organisations.

As a business with a culture of embracing trying out new product offerings they had enjoyed extending the capabilities of their systems with multiple Salesforce Communities[148] to support secondments, partners, projects, classes, etc. You name it! Despite this keenness to try out new things, they ended up lagging behind with making their users more efficient and effective. There were too many manual processes and getting new users up to speed was quite an effort. (This trait is something I see quite often; leaving your poor users behind when they really need some uplifting of their interface, automation, connecting of disjointed areas, simplification…)

---

148   "Community Cloud", Salesforce, https://www.salesforce.com/uk/products/community-cloud/overview/

"Right. We've been set the challenge of streamlining Salesforce usage to reduce waste and burden for our users," Hirsh was addressing the team who looked after the Salesforce instance. "The goal is to reduce the amount of support needed by those users, which means that as well as being good for the users it would also be good for us."

Hirsh looked around at his team and was confident that they were the ones for this job. They worked well together and had collaborated efficiently and effectively for the last two years.

After some discussion, Donatella made a suggestion. "One area which takes loads of effort, so would be a great place to start exploring streamlining opportunities, is the preselection and triage of potential course attendees. The combination of too many steps, a confusing process and a volume of work too big for one user means that the courses presented to potential customers are often less relevant and more error-prone than they should be. If the individuals in the database don't keep their information accurate and up to date this problem is compounded. How about we start there? It's in the interests of those people to keep their own info up to date as it'll mean the courses suggested to them are more relevant."

"Great idea, Dona," Qasim encouraged, "But how do we encourage those individuals to do that?"

Many ideas were put forward to tackle this particular problem. The team decided that the best way forward was to alert individuals for whom there was a potentially interesting match and then take that individual through a series of steps. Those steps would confirm the minimum requirements for the course, update their information, confirm their current status and, if appropriate, apply for the course there and then.

They produced a prototype which looked a bit like an extension of their matching system. It allowed Salesforce users to preselect individuals and send them a notification with relevant information and a call to action. Clicking on the action would open these individuals' personal portals where they would see the course specification and an embedded Lightning Flow[149] would prompt them to read and fill in further information. This would also serve the purpose of updating their record and sending a notification to the user who had preselected them. If these triage questions showed that they didn't meet the base criteria, they would be sent down a path to find more relevant courses.

This was all achieved in a few days of work and low-code approach. Excellent!

Donatella presented their work at show-and-tell and was met with a question. "How about adding in some flexibility which would allow the user to change the questions? Could they make the questions unique to each available course?" It was certainly an interesting idea; all ideas are good, in a sense, and everything is considered as possible.

For that to happen they would need to add an extra layer of complexity, in order to handle the creation of different questions and the possible answers to them. Let's pause for a moment... Was this actually needed? How often does a crafted set of questions and answers for a particular course need to happen? Would doing so mean that the Salesforce user needed to put in more time when sending the notification to the preselected individuals? The goal was to streamline Salesforce usage

---

149   Arnab Rose, "Salesforce Blog: Introducing Lightning Flow", Salesforce, 28/March/18, https://www.salesforce.com/blog/2018/03/introducing-lightning-flow.html

and reduce waste and burden for the users; does this take us away from that?

Just because you **can** do things, doesn't mean that you **should**. And it's okay to challenge, it's actually a good thing and it should be fostered. It's about valuing the individuals and their interactions to enable collaborative ideation, while avoiding shutting it down so you don't miss out.

Self-assess and observe others over the course of the next few discussions that you are involved in. How does a resounding dismissal affect the environment and the following interactions from everyone?

Doing things costs money, time, effort and intelligence. *Doing things* that cost loads but simply don't "do the job" when you only find out at the very end… is a waste. Not only does this kill the budget, but it silently kills the energy levels of everyone involved. Talk about demoralising!

You don't want to be working on something that isn't needed. From lean manufacturing, which comes from Taiichi Ohno[150] and The Toyota Production System, we learn that reducing and eliminating waste is to be the first business objective. As this chapter's principle remarks, it is the art of maximizing the amount of work **not** done.

So keeping things simple allows you not only to finetune to reduce waste, but also to enhance and expand capabilities easily and to amend and refactor the existing ones. In a sense keeping things simple and modular allows you to manage future change less painfully, with minimal impact elsewhere.

"Simplicity speaks with splendour" - Lailah Gifty Akita[151]

---

150   "Taiichi Ohno", Wikipedia, https://en.wikipedia.org/wiki/Taiichi_Ohno

151   "Quote by Lailah Gifty Akita", Good Reads, https://www.goodreads.com/quotes/tag/simple?page=3

Extreme programming encourages starting with the simplest solution. **Simplicity**[152] is another of its values. Keeping things simple that also keeps them modular makes the system easier to understand, extend and evolve over time when and if needed.

---

152   "Extreme Programming", Wikipedia, https://en.wiki-pedia.org/wiki/Extreme_programming#Values

Tip

To reduce waste there are a few things that you can experiment with, firstly that old-school upfront detail planning goes to the bin, bye bye! We can't predict the future and we know that things are going to change, so there is no point in investing time, effort or intelligence in that.

Live by the product vision, constantly revise the direction and work through the upcoming goals collaboratively. Goal-by-goal, cycle-by-cycle, day-by-day.

Instead of that boring upfront detailed planning effort of trying to come up with *the possible future*, you could try mini-brain-storms. Yes, brainstorms! It's an oldie but a goodie to collaborate in ideation. It can be used from product roadmapping to very specific obstacle fighting.

Another term used for this concept is *swarming*. I'd define it as: The act of a group jumping in to solve a problem, get things done, through self organisation and decentralisation. It reminds me of one of the many things we can learn from lean manufacturing, the benefits of leaving roles and hierarchies aside and jumping in as a group with a common goal to work something out.

In lean manufacturing one element is to work together very closely with suppliers for example, with the main purpose of waste reduction, where openness and collaboration goes beyond what we may be used to. That may mean gathering some of your most knowledgeable subject specific people and going to help one of your third parties with an all-hands-on-deck approach. I daresay in Western cultures we do not see or do this enough, we must break through.

Going back to avoiding waste, another tip that helps is to **prioritise ruthlessly!** From the product vision, what are the themes? Out of each theme, what areas compose it? Which one is more important and urgent? Which one would allow us to start trading first?

And kill any *high, medium, low* lists. I am tired of consistently seeing priorities defined this way. Instead have a one dimensional list, where no two items can be the same priority. It's either number one or number two, none of that parallel priorities nonsense.

And last but not least, break it down, real down. What is the bare minimum we can do to prove ourselves wrong or right? The mindset switch of proving ourselves wrong is like injecting steroids to waste reduction. We don't do this enough, it's like developing only happy paths[153] charged with biases and own agendas and we know where that leads. That's why we write negative unit tests[154]. Do the same with your product 'bets'.

---

153   "Happy Path", Wikipedia, https://en.wikipedia.org/wiki/Happy_path

154   "Write Negative Tests Unit", Trailhead, https://trailhead.salesforce.com/en/content/learn/modules/unit-testing-on-the-lightning-platform/negative-tests

Why not try...

To support the art of maximising the amount of work not done, as a team you should be asking yourself with every piece of work: What is the simplest thing that could potentially do the job?

This is also about the tools and functionality we leverage in Salesforce, let me point you to David Lui and Don Robins Play by Play Salesforce Knowing When to Code[155], which covers just this.

Have a bet and get it running *today* rather than something *tomorrow* that won't do the job or will diminish the returns.

This approach allows you to have a control group, so that you can evaluate the difference not only between the existing functionality but who has access or not to the new functionality. For example around marketing we have ingrained the concept

155   Don Robins and David Liu, "Play by Play: Knowing When to Code in Salesforce", Pluralsight, https://app.pluralsight.com/library/courses/play-by-play-salesforce-knowing-when-to-code/table-of-contents

of A/B testing[156] and that being a mail out or a website change, to move away from correlation to causation.

In some scenarios it would make sense to do something similar for your users, so that you can see if the change is bringing out benefits or not. Let's take complaints, these would have happened anyway regardless of the functionality to process them without an escalation.

So for example, you may want to add tracking for how many times a new button is used. Or, if a new feature creates records, have a report that monitors volumes, times, data quality around that.

It's important to be aware that we naturally seek confirmation of our own ideas in the data we collect. Switch this thinking to prove ourselves wrong with the simplest thing, then monitor it closely to decide upon the next micro-step (if any is to be taken).

---

156 "A/B Testing", Wikipedia, https://en.wikipedia.org/wiki/A/B_testing

Semantics

Try to avoid the word *priority*, it's defined by Google as "the fact or condition of being regarded or treated as more important than others". And as in the chapter "Deliver Working Product Frequently" we saw that importance is only one variable.

The word *priority* is overused, another word that comes with loads of baggage when just 50 years ago it was barely used:

Use over time for: priority

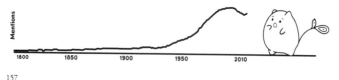

157

Even in the Scrum guide the term *prioritising* has been removed in favour of *ordering*, as a way of referring to organising the Product Backlog.

---

157   "Priority", Google Books Ngram Viewer, http://tiny.cc/
priorityword

Book

The Lean Startup: How Today's Entrepreneurs Use Continuous Innovation to Create Radically Successful Businesses - Eric Ries[158]

This book presents you with the Lean Startup as a movement, to reduce the time of the loop Build-Measure-Learn in the organisation, with the importance of doing the smallest possible and to reduce waste. How to decide when to persevere or when to pivot. The book covers how to test your assumptions as quickly as possible. And all of these being applied in small, medium or large corporations; the concept of a startup being everywhere.

---

158   Eric Ries, *The Movement That Is Transforming How New Products Are Built And Launched*, (Great Britain: Penguin Business, 2011)

Self-Organisation

"The best architectures, requirements, and designs emerge from self-organizing teams." - Agile Manifesto[159]

Jim Highsmith, "History: The Agile Manifesto", Agile Manifesto, 2001, https://agilemanifesto.org/history.html

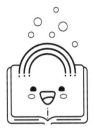

Like a Breath of Fresh Air

Jade and Kwasi looked at their company with pride. Every employee they spoke to felt valued and relevant; the teams had a way of working together which showed strong bonds and effective synergy.

It hadn't always been like this.

Their company was focussed on business to consumer commerce transactions. It had had good financial backing as a startup and had grown rapidly. Four years from its inception, the company now had over two million customers. Wow.

As the company had grown, so had the team. Jade and Kwasi had organically added to the roster over the years, as the volume of work had increased, and their original team of four was now over forty strong.

If you've read this book from the beginning, you should be able to picture how some of the concepts we've already come across might look with a team of that size. For example, over time their planning sessions had become half-day marathons. They had so many tasks to run through that there was only enough time to raise a handful of questions and challenges and it had become almost impossible to predict any feasible outcomes in their cycle.

The team who looked after their Salesforce instance also looked after many other applications related to the customer, from brand engagement across multiple channels through to product payment processing and fulfilment. Salesforce was at its core as the customer master place.

"Is it reasonable to deliver these hundreds of items of such varied nature?" Jade was starting to wonder.

This question was generally followed by a licked finger up in the air, "Yeah... Sure..." Yet, cycle after cycle, there was spillover of work and Kwasi was starting to worry about the commitment levels of some of the team.

In fairness to the team members, their work was presented as a never-ending task list. You could see this manifested in their daily alignment, and reflected in rushed status reports which at times just seemed like a meaningless game of bingo—"Working on 532, BINGO!"—rather than something run by and for the team to add value.

Using the excuse of the new year coming up and having to craft the organisation's vision for the year ahead, Jade and Kwasi brought the team together to discover the themes of work that were in the pipeline. They held a session where fifteen themes of work were presented; for each area they all discussed the benefits and how it contributed to the company vision.

In the next part of the session, the full team of forty people each then ranked these themes from 1 to 15 based on their skills and their interests, 1 being assigned to the area they were most interested in getting involved with and 15 the least. They then grouped the fifteen different themes by context and desired delivery quarters ahead.

Lastly, they self-appointed and defined the teams that would tackle each of the grouped bundles of work. From the ranking exercise it became obvious that there were some more interesting bundles than others, so they reshuffled things for a fair balance.

This was the team that Jade and Kwasi looked at now. The team was a team! A team which functioned so smoothly that no one wanted to mess it up. By organising themselves into more manageable focus groups, they knew they could evolve the architecture, requirements and designs from each one of the grouped themes, because the direction had been set as a group. They had ownership over the value of the products they were delivering and were empowered and motivated by this process.

One of the things that organisations struggle with is growing at scale. We've already seen how communication lines grow at a significantly faster rate than the growth of the team (See Page 142).

So instead of forcing top-down organisational charts, which in my opinion is an outdated archaic legacy tool from the 1800s and hasn't evolved, embrace organic growth with interrelated responsible teams that are autonomous and self-organised.

"Greatness can't be imposed; it has to come from within. But it does live within all of us" - Jeff Sutherland[160]

Think about management rather than dictation. Be there to serve, to unblock obstacles, not to tell people what to do and how to do it (which would be rather narrow-minded with no room for improvement or innovation). Be there to enable an environment where all skills are needed, with multiple devel-

---

160   Jeff Sutherland, *Scrum: The Art of Doing Twice the Work in Half the Time*, (London: Random House Business Books, 2015)

opment products overlapping, limiting bottlenecks, reducing many hand-offs and waiting time.

"We cannot overcome what we ignore" - Cleo Wade[161]

Enabling self-organisation, which is creating an environment where grouplets are able to move from manager-led to self-governing. We must be system aware, how can we organise grouplets to cut down dependencies? To reduce bottlenecks from other technology, departments or roles?

So we can have **commitment** to each other in achieving the goals, being collectively stronger. Another of the Scrum Values, sharing a sincere intent to accept responsibly and follow through, in joint agreement towards the shared goals.

---

161   Cleo Wade, "Want to change the world? Start by being brave enough to care", Ted Women, November/17, https://www.ted.com/talks/cleo_wade_want_to_change_the_world_start_by_being_brave_enough_to_care#t-299411

Tip

From the DevOps State Report 2019 we learn that the research shows that heavyweight change approval processes negatively impact speed and stability. In contrast, having a clearly understood process for changes drives speed and stability, as well as reduction in burnouts.

That is where you want to get to. Even just thinking about the waste of change requests, approval processes, stage gates, go/no-go meetings... even if that's just accounting for the time of people involved, sigh!

Right, here is the deal: you slowly but surely can break through this way of thinking. Take any process as a guide not a doctrine, especially the ones **you** put in place. And within your immediate environment look at how to enable a self-organised team towards what each individual is interested in and has the skills and knowledge to contribute to.

I, personally, quite like to *throw people into a room* but that may not be the best next step for your environment or team size. There may be some themes of work towards which people can pair up or volunteer to champion. Be cautious this doesn't become siloed.

In any scenario remember the power of showing the product and showing it to everyone. In the story one of the things the team of over forty didn't want to lose was the sight of their wider product and architecture, across both Salesforce and the other customer applications. To enable that they had in place some intense demo and brainstorming sessions, a space where everyone was able and expected to contribute.

Why not try...

I've already mentioned the daily alignment to fine-tune and adjust towards that cycle's common goal that the team has committed to. But what could that look like?

To enable that daily alignment, there is the common practice of *a daily stand up*[162] also known as a daily Scrum or simply 'daily'.

It's a fifteen minute catch up *for* and *by* the team to align the next twenty-four hours towards their common goal. It happens every day, in the same place and at the same time when typically the team answers the questions: what have we achieved since the last daily, what are we planning to tackle until the next daily, and do we foresee any blockers to doing so?

It's not a status report. It's not a sign to start the day or act as a wake up alarm. It's not a place for someone to assign work to others. Nope! That would defeat the object of optimising collaboration, self-organisation and performance.

---

162   "The Scrum Guide", Scrum, https://www.scrumguides.org/scrum-guide.html#events-daily

In terms of obstacles raised it's a great place where others offer their helping hand, either in an area of the system about which they may have some knowledge or ideas but also to relationships that can help to reach and branch out to other teams if that's where the obstacles to overcome are.

It's all about favouring finishing over starting stuff. Things that are done and in-use add value, having more things in-progress does not.

Also, for your notes, even though dailies most commonly happen in the morning, it can happen at any time of the day, whatever works best for the team and whatever they agree to. As long as it's every day, at the same time and in the same place, hence the phrasing of the three questions/answers that each contributor covers; reinforcing progress, plans and obstacles towards a common goal. Dailies are the place to tune and adjust so that the goal is achieved, therefore reducing natural deviation.

The name *standup* comes from the desire to keep this as a quick realignment, if we stand up we activate more of our body, mind and soul; and we also feel less comfortable and therefore motivated to keep the meeting to the point. I have even tried daily *forearm planks*, where you can imagine the setting, same content, and that really helped to keep it concise and within the timebox of fifteen minutes.

Here's another experiment that supports self-organisation. Just like in the story when preparing the themes of work (goodie bundles). Throw the people into a room and allow them to self-organise in cross-functional teams. As people may not be used to this, give it a frame so there is no need to start from a blank canvas, map out the areas and the skills needed for each goodie bundle. Even with the frame, this one may be a bit of an advanced experiment for some teams as you need to layer some foundations to get the most out of it.

There you go, you get two experiment ideas in this chapter!

Semantics

Self-organisation doesn't happen overnight and there is lots of stuff within the surrounding environment to influence that to truly happen.

On a team scale it's important to change the narrative of the value and benefits of the work ahead, to reinforce the reason for being and purpose. Also to find out about what interests there are not just within the team but on an individual level, the strength in skills and the desired ones to acquire.

Such fundamentals of value, benefits, interests… we seem to neglect to even acknowledge at times. Do talk about it, there are some frames and techniques to surface the above, but just the simple exercise of mentioning it and reviewing it often, I believe makes a difference.

In terms of semantics I want to mention another one to keep an eye on, and this is very specific to the *daily* alignment. Routines are good for many reasons but can be also damaging as it can lead to falling into auto-pilot, not being fully present. That's a killer in the alignment if people are not really there.

I see it often, people who have heard about the concept of daily standups and go through the motions without the emotions, covering things like, "Yesterday, what did I do? Well, I was

off and today continue working on ticket 324, no blockers."
Tell me, what is the value in that?! How can anyone chip in to
collaborate on such an input? Now, one of the antidotes is the
words that we use, so talk about:

1. What have I *finished* since the last daily.

2. What am I planning to *achieve* before the next one.

3. Do I foresee anything — maybe external or an unknown somewhere in the technology — which might
   block or slow down my progress?

Book

Fish!: A remarkable way to boost morale and improve results - Stephen C. Lundin, Harry Paul and John Christensen[163]

A good all time book, small, easy to read and fun. It talks about the story of Pike Place Fish in Seattle, a popular market stall selling fresh fish for decades as employees playfully throw fish around. It reflects and equates the concepts to any other industry. I find myself looking back at the concepts of this book often, again life is too precious to go through it miserably, in anything one does.

---

163   Stephen C. Lundin, Harry Paul and John Christensen, *Fish! A remarkable Way to Boost Morale and Improve Results*, (London: Hodder & Stoughton Ltd., 2000), https://www.fishphilosophy.com/fish-book/

Inspect and Adapt

"At regular intervals, the team reflects on how to become more effective, then tunes and adjusts its behavior accordingly." - Agile Manifesto[164]

---

164   J. Highsmith, "History: The Agile Manifesto", Agile Manifesto, 2001, https://agilemanifesto.org/history.html

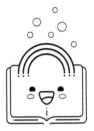

You Can't Make an Omelette
Without Breaking a Few Eggs

A retail company who used Salesforce as their primary sales tool and to support most of their business to business (B2B) agreements, had seen a steady decline in their sales deals over six months. Chris, the Sales Director, was worried.

Their Salesforce org had been stagnant for a few years and, aside from few integrations and a bit of logic, there wasn't much done on the front-end for the users—not even basic report training.

They often discussed the steady decline in sales and it was a source of general worry across the organisation. To try to help to turn this around Chris decided to get Floyd and Spencer from the team who looked after their Salesforce instance and offer to do some training and hands-on sessions.

The two of them put their heads together to plan the sessions they'd deliver. "We need to gear the sessions towards showing these users how to get the most out of the application," was Floyd's starting point.

"Absolutely," agreed Spencer. "We need to make sure we include reporting, so the sales team can go deeper and analyse their accounts."

"Great start! They also need to understand churning and product holdings so that they can understand how to prioritise their efforts when it comes to strategising about how to turn around the current downward trend that they're experiencing," added Floyd.

These ideas seemed to be quite well received by the users at the retail company. Floyd and Spencer also encouraged the team to bring their own suggestions about what they wanted to cover. They built on each other's ideas before deciding to eschew traditional training and go all in for an experiment—a war room[165] style week with the sales, commercial, leadership and Salesforce teams.

They spent a full week in their war room running different ideas which might help them to reach potential sales. After every few attempts Chris would encourage the team to reflect on how it had gone, considering a whole range of things. What information would have been useful? What didn't work? What did? How could they try things differently next time?

By reflecting with a range of questions, they gained a range of insights. Some of the things that were identified through this process were down to the specific approach they had taken. Some were about access to contextual information whilst on a call. Some concerned external information. Sometimes it was the tone and words

---

165   A war room is "a room in the building of a...business organization equipped with the technical means to gather information, plan strategy, direct activities, etc.", "War room", CollinsDictionary, https://www.collinsdictionary.com/dictionary/english/war-room

used... you name it. They were uncovering so many different reflections which was making everyone in the room more aware, smarter and stronger.

Chris was able to use some of the feedback to make updates on their Salesforce and deployments on the spot. The motivation this brought combined with more experiments, more reflections, more adjustments. There was a vibrant energy in the room.

Importantly, not every idea or insight needed a deployment; one of the great eye openers for the sales team was when Floyd introduced them to list views[166]. "It's like having a superpower!" exclaimed Emilio, one of the sales team. "I can use this to help myself in so many ways! I can see how this will help me to visualise, organise and prioritise my effort and take immediate action. This is brilliant!"

"The more the team, practices making responsible action & learning towards proactive goals, the more resilient they are to the accelerating change" - Ross Mayfield[167]

Having regular check-ins to align direction is super powerful. The ability to tune and adjust reduces waste and deviation and realignment. Markets change, visions change, technologies change, teams change, settings change, relationships change... with an ever-changing environment it would be naive to think that you can draw the future with a straight line.

---

166   "Create and Customize List Views", Trailhead, https://trailhead.salesforce.com/en/content/learn/modules/lex_customization/lex_customization_list

167   Ross Mayfield, "Continuous Alignment of Product Management", Product Coalition, 9/November/18, https://productcoalition.com/continuous-alignment-of-product-management-699bd61c2c0b

Often what I observe in teams' reflections is that what is covered is about *what is being done*, but we seem to unconsciously skip *how it's been done*. Let's illustrate simplistically what happens if we do not pay attention to the *how*:

The *how* are many things from the interactions, the self-organisation, to the elevation of systematic repetitive efforts, down to maximising the value.

There you have it, the grand difference of effectiveness and efficiency. We can do really well and go really fast with little return, instead we should concentrate on delivering the intended results. And that requires failing a lot and learning from it. Think of it as just like scientific research.

Once again looking at the Toyota Production System, at any point any grouplet could stop the production line and yes, it's in the context of manufacturing, so imagine the implications of stopping the production line for one team to figure out together what's going wrong and solve it right there and then. Mechanical, hardware, software, you name it... you can extrapolate the principle; an open and honest environment about mistakes, where the entire system can learn, that's how one gains improvements.

Thinking of such small improvements would be exhausting if not impossible, coming from the leadership team. Hence it has to happen on a micro-level, within the team, to control their own product and their own destiny. They are the closest so, naturally, they know more about it.

For that to happen there is a lot of undoing we need to do to move away from a top-down approach. Command and control is archaic and it just doesn't work, plus it is slow and does it ever really enable any deep change? We must move away from blame and hierarchy and instead foster an ongoing process of trial-and-error whereby learning and self-correction is part of the operating system. An evolution, not a revolution.

Another layer that I frequently observe, especially for teams that don't have reflections often, is that team reflections come *after the fact*. Our memories are not strictly made of clear and specific facts about how something happened. In hindsight we seem to remember and understand things very differently depending on the outcome[168].

Without failure there is no learning and without learning there is no progress. Failure is an opportunity to learn and as any opportunity you either grab it or miss it.

There is the tendency to self-obstruct learning from mistakes, as if it were a 'one off', an 'it happens', a 'we quickly fixed it', or a 'no one noticed'... By doing so, we sabotage our own progress by dismissing, hiding and even editing failure.

Look at successful products, companies, teams and individuals. To me there is a pattern there, a pattern about how they detect and respond to failure. They do it with an ongoing adaptive process, where failure is part of the journey as it is in science, and the learning is the steering wheel.

"Drive out fear, so that everyone may work effectively for the company." - Dr. Edwards Deming[169]

---

168   Elizabeth A. Kensinger, "Remembering the Details: Effects of Emotion." *Emotion review: journal of the International Society for Research on Emotion* vol. 1,2 (2009): 99-113. https://www.ncbi.nlm.nih.gov/pmc/articles/PMC2676782/

169   John Hunter, "Where There is Fear You Do Not Get Honest Figures", Deming, 28/February/13 https://blog.deming.org/2013/02/where-there-is-fear-you-do-not-get-honest-figures/

We need to nurture an environment where it is safe to fail, with experimentation as part of the path, with resilience. As we know, things don't always go as expected, and that is to be expected. Pushing the boundaries of knowledge from what proved us wrong, with the courage to reveal flags, admit errors, the humility to test early and adapt rapidly.

In a sense, the Salesforce concept of a business tool in an organisation brings openness and collaboration, this being one of the reasons that drew me to stick with it. Where you have access and work together within context to close that deal, to report yourself on the current matter of affairs, easy and real-time access to the data that is according to plan or not; so that you can finetune your efforts rather than continuing on a path of deviation from reality.

The last value of Extreme Programming and Scrum that we have not yet covered is **Respect**[170]. As usual, it should start with oneself, and of course extend to others. In everything we do, such as a new deployment, don't 'break' others' work or 'break' unit tests and do respect that nobody on the team should feel unappreciated or ignored. It's about understanding that we all are capable, independent and interdependent people with voices worth being heard.

170   "Extreme Programming", Wikipedia, https://en.wikipedia.org/wiki/Extreme_programming#Values

Tip

So how can we create an environment where reflection is part of what we do? Spin your own version of a retrospective[171].

In the Scrum framework the retrospective is one of the events that is part of the process (I argue here that it should be part of the everyday, regardless of whether you do use Scrum or not). You typically do this at the end of every iteration, let's say on Fridays. It's a time to pause and reflect and act as that learning opportunity.

A retrospective is an internal event where all team members gather to catch up and review how the iteration went, why was it that way, collaborate with ideas to make it better and agree which ones the team has the energy and is ready to give it a try next week. It should also be a way to make cycle after cycle less painful, more productive and more fun to work.

Unfortunately this is one of the events that gets dropped the most, but why is that? Maybe because it's hard! It requires a maturity level and trust, it requires coming out of the comfort zone until it becomes the comfort zone. It calls for peo-

---

171 "The Scrum Guide", ScrumGuides, https://www.scrumguides.org/scrum-guide.html#events-retro

ple to feel and make others feel safe, to bring up stuff that bothers them as solution-oriented rather than moaning or a finger-pointing way.

"Learn from the mistakes of others. You can't live long enough to make them all yourself" - Eleanor Roosevelt[172]

It's not a lesson learnt, it's a timebox that experiments with the process itself. Again, the goal is not to do 'Agile', the goal is to improve. And improvements can happen at any point, the retrospective acts as a reminder and a formal pause to 'pause', introspect, retrospect and adjust accordingly to become more effective, towards delivering better value sooner, safer and happier.

This pause needs to be well looked after so that it doesn't become daunting. I've written an article[173] with a few ideas on how to frame it and a few tips if you want to read further. With time you and the team will have a few techniques, styles and antipatterns to watch out for in your toolkit.

---

172 "Quote by Eleanor Roosevelt", Good Reads, https://www.goodreads.com/quotes/6521824-learn-from-the-mistakes-of-others-you-can-t-live-long

173 Ines Garcia, "Why Team Reflection is Important", LinkedIn, 10/April/20, https://www.linkedin.com/pulse/why-team-reflection-important-ines-garcia/

Why not try...

We have all been there, done something which has gone a little quirky, then quickly tried to reverse and resolve it, stressing the hell out and holding our breath. It's not a nice place to be. Yet when it's all over, we let it be a 'one off' and say to ourselves that we solved it and then no one has to know, 'don't worry it's all sorted'. I wonder even if we really acknowledged, understood and learnt from it?

It's exhausting, putting all your brain power into a highly demanding environment in a short time span (if you are lucky). Once it's over you are relieved and yet deflated. That's your body trying to level it up.

Here's a bonus story. On a team that I've worked with this pattern became a common occurrence, and by the nature of the set up we had little crossover time together as a team. The worst part was that many of the 'oops mistakes' were reoccurring. It became so apparent that we invented 'F*cked it up' certificates. So every time one of these things happened we awarded ourselves one of these certificates, with a message to our future selves. This gave us the opportunity as a team to pause and share the learning, either we solved it by ourselves or with others. We even displayed them in the office. A permanent reminder, some of which became future backlog work.

A mistake without learning is a waste. Instead, making mistakes whilst we learn and sharing that wisdom, is where the value is. We must be open about them and collaborate on that knowledge gain. No secret quick fixes, we know that these will bite us in the butt.

Build on each other's successes and failures instead of hijacking progress.

"You learn through solving problems, failing, reflecting on failure, and adjusting course." - Steve Jobs[174]

---

174   John Shook, "What's Your Problem?", Lean, 31/October/18, https://www.lean.org/shook/DisplayObject.cfm?o=4803

Semantics

One way to express that failure is to embed it as part of the process, and one way to relieve fear of failure is to encourage experiments. Just like our question "Are you willing to give it a try?" it works a treat to reduce resistance to progress. By calling them experiments, we set the expectation that some will not work, and that's okay.

But they exist so you can learn. If you don't, you get stuck. We must change how we think about failure, it's part of the journey to discovery as it is with science.

"Sometimes the effort spent avoiding a mistake can exceed the cost of making the mistake" - Mike Cohn[175]

---

175   Mike Cohn, "The Optimal Number of Mistakes is Not Zero", Weekly Tips Newsletter, 6/December/18

Book

Black Box Thinking: Marginal Gains and the Secrets of High Performance - Matthew Syed[176]

We often talk about the importance of failure and the psychological safety that should be present at work. This book goes deep into the imperative need not only to change our mindset but the reasons why there is resistance to open and transparent environments with constant eagerness to evolve from their mistakes, also being part of the process. It covers how and why the concept behind the black box exists in aviation and how and why it's similar or missing in other industries, also to why and what could be done about it.

---

176   Matthew Syed, *Black Box Thinking: The Surprising Truth About Success*, (London: John Murray, 2015)

Who Moved My Cheese? An Amazing Way to Deal with Change in Your Work and in Your Life - Dr Spencer Johnson[177]

A bonus recommendation. An all time motivational business fable, a short and simple story of two mice and two people covering the importance of adapting to change of environment rather than waiting and expecting things to come to you. Although it may sound simplistic it has a clear and strong message which you can extrapolate and observe in everyday interactions within organisations.

---

177   Dr. Spencer Johnson, *Who Moved My Cheese: An Amazing Way to Deal with Change in Your Work and in Your Life,* (London: Ebury Publishing, 1999)

Where do we begin?

We are coming to the end, and we have covered a hell of a lot of different concepts, stories, learnings, experiments, semantics… I hope that by now you have already observed and tweaked some things in your own environment. Even though it may seem like a lot of stuff to do, try to influence for a *mindset shift* without generating much noise nor argument.

When we humans learn new things, we trust who is teaching us. Yet, at the same time, we are unsure about how to use the new learnings by ourselves. Because of this it also becomes harder to explain the new learnings to others so that we can use them beyond ourselves. It's not only about explaining the concepts recently learned but it's also about putting them into practice.

To implement new learnings we need to be aware that when something is so powerful that it changes the environment, it is going to need to evolve even faster as it changes the environment where it is applied. Therefore, amplifying the importance of inspecting and adapting on a continuum. We must do this collaboratively, so that knowledge becomes a shared experience that can be enriched with diversity, so that in turn it can disseminate and cross-pollinate.

I often get asked for a detailed breakdown of, let's say, an 18 month step-by-step Agile transformation plan. I hope by now you'd agree that that's missing the point, so when that happens I want to run in the opposite direction as fast as I can. Although instead, I will try to explain why we should be looking at it in a different way.

"The desire for perfection rests upon two fallacies. The first resides in the miscalculation that you can create optimal solutions sitting in a bedroom or ivory tower and thinking things through rather than getting into the real world and testing assumptions, thus finding their flaws. It is the problem of valuing top-down over bottom-up.

The second fallacy is the fear of failure: earlier on we looked at situations where people fail and then proceed to either ignore or conceal those failures. Perfectionism is, in many ways, more extreme. You spend so much time designing and strategizing that you don't get a chance to fail at all, at least until it is too late. It is pre-closed loop behaviour, you are so worried about messing up that you never even get on the field to play." - Matthew Syed[178]

We should always start with the end in mind. It guides our steps, decisions and tweaks whilst we continuously review and adjust direction.

Over the years I've found that the bare minimum one can do is to start towards improvement, which is made up of two simple things:

1. Visual Representation of the Work in Progress

"The idea is that there should be no secret cabal, no hidden agendas, nothing behind the curtain" - Jeff Sutherland[179]

We humans are visual beings, we digest visuals so much faster than words.

178   Matthew Syed, *Black Box Thinking: The Surprising Truth About Success*, (London: John Murray, 2015)

179   Jeff Sutherland, *Scrum: The Art of Doing Twice the Work in Half the Time*, (London: Random House Business Books, 2015)

Let's correlate the concept of 'the power of visuals' to Salesforce. Think about tools like Flows[180] or Process Builder[181] or even the diagram from Approvals[182]. Suddenly you supercharge your conversations by showing the logic in a visual way to any discussion. Images speak louder than words.

These visuals come into play by having a place where all the team's work in progress shows, where it's open and accessible. This surfaces so much more than we would have been able to know without it. It acts as an information radiator[183].

One tool often used is a Kanban board, once again a reference from the Toyota Production System. Kanban[184] is a Japanese word that literally means *visual sign*. From the principle of using visuals so no problems are hidden.

The common practice around this board is to section it in columns such as: To Do, In Progress, Done; this being the bare bones. But you can add more columns to show, for example, handoffs and highlight detailed bottlenecks.

---

180   "Guide Users Through Your Business Processes With Flow Builder", Trailhead, https://trailhead.salesforce.com/en/content/learn/modules/business_process_automation/flow

181   "Automate Simple Business Processes With Process Builder", Trailhead, https://trailhead.salesforce.com/en/content/learn/modules/business_process_automation/process_builder

182   "Customize How Records Get Approved with Approvals Unit", Trailhead, https://trailhead.salesforce.com/en/content/learn/modules/business_process_automation/approvals

183   "Information Radiators", Agile Alliance, www.agilealliance.org/glossary/information-radiators

184   "Kanban", Wikipedia, https://en.wikipedia.org/wiki/Kanban

It also helps to measure things like:

- lead time (average total time between idea creation and its delivery)

- cycle time (average time to finish one unit).

Especially if you have a digital format tool for it; these things are generally baked into it.

And although it may be in a digital format, it doesn't have to lose the power of being an information radiator. Have it displayed in the grouplet workspace and open for everyone to see.

This visual of work in progress acts to convey agreement, to trigger conversations, to surface information and encourage alignment.

It is there where you gather daily with your team during each cycle. So avoid overloading that visual, keep it neat and focused on the immediate, therefore preventing it from overwhelming and becoming a burden to the team. It is there to aid.

A visual representation of work in progress will unfold when things are added or removed, how often and where they came from. It will make obvious when a team is over or under loaded and it will also prompt to level up the efforts; as well as to encourage collaboration and swarming when needing to get things out the door between all members.

It will become apparent where the blockers, obstacles and bottlenecks are, as well as what's slowing the team down. Remember to favour finishing over starting work; done work brings value, having many things in progress does not.

And as with everything, start with yourself. You can use it for your personal life, run a couple of weeks of experiments with a visual representation of your 'to dos'. This will give you the foundation to articulate to your team, that you have read about the power of visual representation of work and you have experimented with it, share your findings and then ask, "are you willing to give it a try?". There is nothing to lose and so much potential to gain.

"I wouldn't ask anyone to do anything I wouldn't do myself" - Indra Nooyi[185]

The visuals will bring so much to the surface that will be screaming for reflection.

So here is the second thing as a bare minimum to start the journey to become more Agile whilst delivering Salesforce:

2. Pause, get curious & adapt

We get so entangled in our **busyness** that we don't give ourselves the ability to see with perspective. That grand difference between efficiency and effectiveness. So we keep going harder, faster, stronger… and without headspace, that doesn't always end up well.

Taking the concepts from our prior chapter. Of course reflection and adaptation on the spot is the nirvana, but we know that doesn't always happen.

Make time for both yourself and your team's headspace, as part of the process until it becomes a habit, do it at regular intervals.

---

185   Indra Nooyi, "25 Inspirational Quotes by Powerful Women", Forbes, https://www.forbes.com/pictures/hfej45mgk/indra-nooyi-ceo-pepsic/

Reflect on how you can become effective, and experiment with ideas that will emerge from that reflection.

It doesn't have to be formal, it doesn't have to be serious, and it certainly shouldn't be daunting. It does require openness and humility, a deep understanding and readiness that we all can become better.

In that 'pause' time get curious about how it went: your last cycle, your last week, your 'this very day'. Get curious about how it can become.

And do so collectively, so that you can enrich your understanding with others' experiences and perspectives. Great ideas surface from building upon each other. Design participation to include everyone, some people may be more vocal than others. Diversity of opinions augments our sight, our thinking, it strengthens our products and improves our lives.

Don't get disheartened when things don't work. *Trial and error* are part of the process. There will be times when we need more trials than others. Experiment with your process to pursue a happier life, with our days being perishable the least we can do is get the most out of them for a better tomorrow.

And with all of this, slowly but surely, finding areas to help the individual, the team and the organisation to grow.

Let's not forget our partners and customers also; the journey to become better should include everyone. Another learning from the Toyota Production System, with the principles of creating a continuous process to flow / bring problems to the surface and to build a culture of stopping to fix problems.

The concept of partnership is really that, working together with total transparency. Which may lead at times to you jumping in to help your partner, physically going to their offices or whatever may be required, perhaps bringing the field experts to the subject in question from your end. Challenge and help your network of partners, including suppliers, to improve and expect no less from them.

Become a learning organisation, team and individual through persistent reflection and constant improvements.

Starting as a grouplet, an agile bubble, is perfectly fine. To go through the motions *with* emotions will get the attention from adjacent environments. People get curious and that is when the agile bubble will start to expand.

We cannot solve the problems around us with the very same way of thinking that we used when we created them in the first place.

"A new type of thinking is essential if mankind is to survive and move toward higher levels."- Albert Einstein[186]

It's all about slicing and dicing step-by-step and taking one thing at a time. You can actually change the world.

---

186   Albert Einstein, "Atomic Education Urged by Einstein", New York Times, 25/May/46

Acknowledgements

This book wouldn't be possible without the experience with so many teams and their openness, care, attention and thrive. Thank you for all those comments, questions, ideas and challenges to the status quo.

Embarking on this journey to write a book was rather an unknown territory for me, and being completely honest it was also a bit scary. For their guidance and advice on what becoming an author entails, I want to thank: Karen Mangia VP of Customer & Market Insights at Salesforce, Andrew Fawcett VP Product Management at Salesforce, and Salesforce MVPs Eliot Harper, Rafael Hernandez, Deepa Patel, Enrico Murru, Rakesh Gupta and Johan Yu.

Deeply thankful to Karen Moran for your eye for detail, care, creativity, honesty and wit; you helped me reflect and elevate the stories so their messages could be heard, it's been truly a pleasure working with you. And Daniel Shale thank you for your support and questions, my favourite moment was when you asked me to explain Version Control, which I did within the context of our collaborative document for writing this book, then you came back saying: "*Makes sense, I had no idea! Thank god for automated version control!*".

A very special thank you to Chris Edwards, a great friend who I met thanks to the Salesforce Trailblazer community, who is supportive beyond comprehension and who has kindly acted as my private patient editor for a while. And Talal Al-Tamimi whose advice, review and wise words I truly appreciate. This book would not make half a sense without both of your inputs.

People often ask me how I get to contribute to so many initiatives and how I get to do so many different things. There are multiple factors that enable that to happen, but none of it would be possible without the endless support, patience and love from my wife Helen. This book is no different, she has been a pillar from its inception. Helen, I can't thank you enough for your revisions, corrections, encouragement, challenges, support and ideas. Thank you for walking together with me in this journey called life.

More from Ines

Thank you for reading my book. Now that you've seen what I have to say about Salesforce and Agile, I think it's about time I tell you a bit more about myself.

I grew up in Barcelona where I studied a communications double-degree (five years) with an emphasis on advertising, PR and marketing. I'm a fan of board games and an advocate for mindful, healthy living. That said, I'm also a Salesforce nerd[187] and Agile (as you can probably tell).

I'm an Agile Coach, a Certified Scrum Professional® (CSP-SM) and a Salesforce MVP. Altogether, I help organisations every day to become more Agile whilst delivering Salesforce technology. I consult, speak and train in these arenas always

---

187   If you want to know more about how exactly I got into Salesforce, read my article: https://salesforceweek. ly/2017/11/why-is-salesforce-awesome.html

with the end in mind of empowering an Agile mindset evolution (not revolution).

As of the writing of this book I hold 10 active Salesforce certifications and since 2013 I have delivered numerous Sales Cloud, Service Cloud, Community Cloud, Pardot, Apps, Social Studio, Marketing Cloud solutions to a variety of organisations on Salesforce technology. I'm an active member and collaborator on ScrumAlliance.org and AgileAlliance.org.

If you liked this book you may also like some of my experiments and ideas. Head over to www.getagile.co.uk, where you'll see one of my recent inventions being a game for teams to self-assess and have a laugh www.theagileretrospectivegame.com

I'd like to stay in touch with you. If you haven't yet, subscribe to my newsletter *www.getagile.co.uk/join* on my website. You can also follow me on Twitter (*@inescapinezka*) and on LinkedIn (*in/InesGarciaAgile*).

If you write a review of this book somewhere I'd love to know what you think, please tag me and add the book hashtag *#SalesforceAgile*.

FREE DOWNLOAD

No more finger in
the air
guesstimates.

Printed in Great Britain
by Amazon

55220346R00132